MUSIC WITH ESN CHILDREN
A guide for the classroom teacher

Pamela I. Dickinson

NFER Publishing Company Ltd

Published by the NFER Publishing Company
2 Jennings Buildings, Thames Avenue,
Windsor, Berks. SL4 1QS
Registered Office: The Mere, Upton Park, Slough, Berks. SL1 2DQ
First published 1976
© Pamela Dickinson
ISBN 0 85633 085 X

Typeset by Jubal Multiwrite Ltd.,
66 Loampit Vale, London SE13 7SN,
Printed in Great Britain by
John Gardner (Printers) Ltd.,
Hawthorne Road, Bootle, Merseyside L20 6JX
Distributed in the USA by Humanities Press Inc.,
Hillary House-Fernhill House, Atlantic Highlands,
New Jersey 07716 USA

Contents

LIST OF TABLES AND FIGURES

PREFATORY NOTE

Dr Dickinson's Modified Battery of Musical Ability Tests forms an integral part of this book. A cassette recording of the four Tests is available from the NFER Publishing Company, 2 Jennings Buildings, Thames Avenue, Windsor, Berks. SL4 1QS.

In the preparation of the Test Battery, the writer must acknowledge the work of previous educators, and in particular, the tests of Dr Arnold Bentley.

Special thanks must also go to all the teachers and children who participated in the study, and especially to the Headmaster, teachers and pupils at 'Dunbar' Special School for ESN Children.

Main quotations are included with grateful acknowledgement to the following authors and publishers: The Schools Music Association (1964) 'Report on Music in Special Schools', pp. 3—4, reprinted by permission of the Association, Bromley, Kent; Richard Colwell (1970) *The Evaluation of Music Teaching and Learning*, pp. 75—76, reprinted by permission of Prentice-Hall, Inc., Englewood Cliffs, New Jersey, USA; J.P.B. Dobbs (1966) *The Slow Learner and Music: A Handbook for Teachers*, p. 16, reprinted by permission of Oxford University Press, London; B.S. Bloom, D.R. Krathwohl and B.B. Masia (1964) *Taxonomy of Educational Objectives, Handbook II: Affective Domain*, David McKay Company, New York, *passim* pp. 122—30, 177; E.W. Eisner 'Instructional and Expressive Educational Objectives: Their Formulation and Use in Curriculum', pp. 15—16, in J.W. Popham, *et al.* (1969) *Instructional Objectives*, Rand McNally, Chicago; J.P. Rowntree (1960) 'A Critical Evaluation of the Bentley "Measures of Musical Abilities", with Particular Reference to Practice Effect on Various of the Sub-tests', MEd dissertation, University of Newcastle-upon-Tyne, pp. 217, 244;

Finally we should mention that in this book, whenever musical notes are named in roman capitals (F, C, etc.), *generally* no specific octave pitch is signified; if, however, specific pitches *are* being identified (according to the system mentioned in fn. 1, p. 50), the context should make this clear.

Chapter One

Music and the ESN Child[1]

A look at the medium
Explanations of such a complex term as 'music' are difficult
to make. However one describes it: whether comparatively,
as a language, for instance, or to quote Langer (1953) 'a tonal
analogue of emotive life'; whether conceptually, like Alston
(1972) 'the tonal representation of sentient and emotional
reality in non-discursive articulate forms'; or whether
describing music purely in terms of its raw materials, to
quote Jacobs (1968) 'the art or science of arranging sounds in
notes and rhythms to give a desired pattern or effect', one
must conclude that the substance of the experience is
'sound'.

It is well known that sound has always been part of man's
life throughout history; the organized sound of music
probably developed originally from the imitation of natural
sounds. Furthermore, music has been associated variously
with magic, religion and healing. Today, recognition of
music's contribution to work with the handicapped has led to
the development of a new subject, music therapy. Alvin
(1966) defines it as 'the controlled use of music in the
treatment, rehabilitation, education and training of adults
and children suffering from physical, mental and emotional
disorder'. Erickson's definition (1970), bearing on the
educable mentally retarded,[2] is more specific, still: 'Musically
elicited behaviour designed to eliminate disorder in the
retardate's cognitive field'.

---

1 Definitions of educational subnormality are discussed in Chapter Three.
2 An American term roughly equivalent to ESN.

In the present study we are not interested in definitions *per se*. It is sufficient to recognize that music can have a therapeutical effect on any listener or performer simply because it provides opportunities for emotional release, self-expression and non-verbal communication. According to Gilman and Paperte (1952) the human organism can be stimulated at all levels by tone and rhythm: the hypothalamic (instinctual responses); the cerebellar (co-ordination and bodily rhythm); the cortical (imagery and association); and the psychic (creative or aesthetic response). In other words, music can affect people of widely varying personality, background, intelligence and attainment.

In this knowledge there is promise for the ESN child. Nonetheless we may well ask, why include music in the curriculum of an ESN school? This is a question of obvious interest to educators, and we shall attempt to provide some answers to it in the next section.

The value of music to the ESN child

It appears from a review of the literature, which is as yet small, that music with subnormals, as with children handicapped in other ways, is most valued for its non-musical benefits. The attitude of educationalists, here and abroad, is well expressed in the remarks of Graham (1972), Alvin (1965) and the Department of Education and Science (1969a). Graham, who views music as fitting into the total curriculum for educable mentally retarded children, suggests that the special music education programme *encourages* the development of skills aimed at in the general EMR programme (i.e. skills needed to gain employment and to become a happy and responsible adult), through providing opportunities not only for aesthetic expression but also for social growth. Alvin, similarly, considers that music's value to the subnormal child lies in its non-academic application, as an aid to his general development. According to the Department of Education and Science, music's importance to the personal and social development of the child needing special education cannot be overemphasized. They point to the long-term potential of this interest which can lead to social integration in adulthood; the mental stimulation which can carry over to other areas; the possibility of immediate appeal, enabling presentation at the child's chronological or mental age. For the ESN pupil, in particular, music is viewed as a field for exploration which can aid the growth of personality.

One finds many similar references throughout the literature. As a point of interest, here is a list of the more notable benefits which have been claimed for doing music with ESN children:

1. the experience of emotional satisfaction;
2. improved concentration, extension of attention span;
3. the experience of self-confidence;
4. satisfaction of the need to communicate, without the barrier of language;
5. stimulation of reading activity;
6. improved articulation;
7. heightened perceptions;
8. stimulation of interest and curiosity;
9. the satisfaction of achievement;
10. stimulation of group involvement, social awareness and acceptable social behaviour;
11. improved co-ordination and motor control; and
12. stimulation of learning.

To illustrate the last point, we might cite Levin and Levin (1972) who consider music to be an important tool in conveying the primary skills of early learning, i.e. fine and gross motor abilities, sequencing, limit setting, concept of numbers, language development, rote counting and developing laterality. So too, some educators are particularly interested in music's role as a means of reinforcing and integrating other subject-matter areas — see e.g., Reacks (1961).

If we delve further into the literature, we discover several significant facts: that music is a feature in a number of curricula for the retarded — e.g., Connor and Talbot (1964), Carlson and Ginglend (1961), Goldstein and Seigle (*n.d.*), Bereiter and Engelmann (1966); that within the past ten years or so there have been some specific musical studies in the field (much significant work here is connected with the names of Alvin, Bailey, Dobbs, and Nordoff and Robbins). Moreover, there have appeared, though as yet rare, a number of specialized music curricula for the retarded — e.g., Ginglend and Stiles (1965), Robins and Robins (1963), Buker (1966).

Communication is contingent upon the use of and comprehension of symbols, and there are many linguistic systems besides the English language which employ such signs —

algebra, logic, Morse code, computer language, the sign language of the deaf, ballet, and not least, music. If imbeciles can be taught to understand symbols (as the researches of O'Connor and Hermelin indicate, 1963), then the possibilities for such development in ESN children are promising indeed. Speech and reading are prime considerations in any projected educative process, but other avenues of communication might be explored with advantage, the expressive arts in particular. In our own experience, music, both as art and science, has much to offer the retarded, and we can only endorse the education correspondent of the *British Journal of Music Therapy* when she urges (Autumn 1973) that music no longer be treated as a plaything but as a serious subject which can contribute to all areas of learning.

If we agree, then, that music is a good idea, the question naturally arises: how shall we present it? To gain a perspective on this it would be helpful to examine what various educators have proposed.

Some approaches to music with ESN children

A main issue which arises in examining methods concerns attitudes towards differential teacher abilities. On the one hand is the specialized music therapy approach, dependent for application on a trained teacher-therapist, while on the other is the approach which allows for non-specialist direction, for instance by the classroom teacher.

The latter trend is apparent in the curricula, mentioned earlier, which include music as part of their total programmes. Connor and Talbot's experimental curriculum for pre-school educable mentally retarded children (1964) was prepared and used by teachers during four years of experimental sessions at Teachers College, Columbia University. Music was one of several group activities in a programme which aimed at enrichment through 'action' experiences. Included in the music activity were: daily singing; playing percussion instruments (which in some cases were made by the children); and listening and moving to music (including finger plays, body movements, clapping, marching and simple folk dances), the record player being an important focus of attention. During the last two years of the experimental classes, the teachers received help from a music consultant. In the third year they worked weekly with her for an hour: one teacher team (the ratio was two teachers to 15 children) included a pianist whereas the other did not; and one team doubted their ability to carry a tune. The consultant dealt with these problems through direct teaching — explaining basic chords to enable the use of the piano, and finding suitable ranges to enable the relaxed singing of tunes.

The aspect of enriched activity is also central to the ideas of Carlson and Ginglend, whose book (1961) contains details of specific play activity projects designed for young retarded children of six years mental age or younger. Whilst the material, it is noted, could be useful to teachers, it is directed primarily to parents, in other words, the untrained, a readership requiring particular consideration as regards presentation. The authors view their book as a means for growth in that sectional activities are arranged in order of increasing difficulty. Suggested musical activities include songs with actions; rhythms (e.g. marching, rhythm band work); also musical games and folk dancing. As an additional feature, construction details are given for simple instruments which the child himself can make and play.

Goldstein and Seigle's plan for educating the educable mentally handicapped (*n.d.*), includes suggestions for a music programme, to be organized by the teachers, which will comprise rhythmical activities (i.e. movements to music, clapping, rhythm band), and also listening, singing and dancing. Music as a means of integrating other subject-matter areas is also considered. The authors explain that the programme need not be directed by a specialist in music education, provided the teacher has sufficient confidence to sing a simple melody and to operate a record player; they do, however, advise her to seek help from the music consultant in her school system.

In Bereiter and Engelmann's programme for the disadvantaged pre-schooler (1966), music is featured as an adjunct to teaching language. Thus we find a music programme devoted to songs, all specially chosen or rewritten to provide practice in certain language tasks. Methods are detailed very precisely for the teacher, who, it is suggested, should probably be independent of the piano accompanist unless experienced in directing from the piano. The authors propose a music period lasting some 15 or 20 minutes.

Moving on to specific musical studies in the field, we come across several specialist approaches. Alvin who in her *Music for the Handicapped Child* (1965) discusses the problems of various handicaps and the ways in which music can be used, explains that her approach is remedial, a means not an end, and therefore unconcerned with high or perhaps even ordinary standards of achievement. She also points out that methods of music can be adapted to the degree of sub-normality. Several activities are considered: singing, playing instruments (in the main, percussion), and listening, also music and movement, and music reading. A very personal contribution is involved in the listening activity whereby the author gives live performances on the cello. Implicit in Alvin's work is the specialist nature of its application and indeed she states her conviction that truly creative musical experiences for the handicapped child depend on the teacher or therapist possessing psychological knowledge and musical skill.

A very specialized music therapy approach for handi-capped children has been developed by Nordoff in col-laboration with Robbins (1965). The method is based on individual therapy: the therapist improvises at the piano and the child responds on another instrument, in most cases a professional side drum with attached cymbal. It is an approach for trained musician-pianists who have a wide range of musical styles at their fingertips. When the child is encouraged to beat his drum, music is improvised to what he beats; the child reacts to this and the pianist to the child's reaction, and so on. The technique aims at an intensely active experiencing of music.

The investigations of Nordoff and Robbins have also focused on group activities. Their work in this area is detailed in *Music Therapy in Special Education* (1971b), a book written for, amongst others, special education teachers who wish to undertake music with their pupils, and who are proficient enough on an instrument to initiate a programme. Chapters giving advice on singing, resonator bells, in-strumental activities and plays with music draw, to a large extent, on works especially composed by the authors. The suggestions are for a teamwork approach — a pianist and leader working together — though there is also room for a musician-teacher working alone.

A handbook written primarily with the non-specialist in mind is *The Slow Learner and Music* by Dobbs (1966). The author reckons that most of the activities described can be undertaken by any musically sensitive and enthusiastic special education teacher who is willing to devote time and thought to his materials; much, it is claimed, can be learned *with* the pupils, joint progress encouraging joint satisfaction.

General suggestions for activities are discussed in relation to singing, playing instruments, listening to music, and movement and dance. The suggestions are based on work done with teachers in various parts of the country, and are the culmination of a pioneer short course held in Leicester in 1964.[1] Dobbs comments that in doing music with slow learners we are not primarily concerned with training them as musicians but rather with educating them as people ready to participate in community life as happier, more mature personalities.

Much the same sentiments are expressed by the late P. F. C. Bailey, whose book *They Can Make Music* (1973) is concerned with both mentally and physically handicapped children. Again, the non-specialist's needs are recognized, the author expressing the hope his ideas will assist the inexperienced teacher to prepare a suitable programme for her pupils. Simple approaches to singing, notation, instrumental music and other musical activities are discussed, based on Bailey's long experience in the field, and his original work with the physically handicapped, and severely subnormal.

The musical studies we have just considered offer broadly-based information relevant to music with ESN children. Now, we turn to some examples of specific, precisely defined programmes. A practical method designed to assist both the trained and untrained is that of Ginglend and Stiles (1965) whose annotated handbook of songs is planned to appeal to groups of children, large or small, with a mental age of three to eight. The selections, organized under 12 themes of interest to children, include traditional songs, folk songs, adaptations and original compositions, all with piano accompaniments, and including suggestions for actions and the use of rhythmical instruments. The autoharp is recommended as an alternative to the piano, chord indications being given for most of the selections; and directions for playing the autoharp, as well as the rhythmic instruments of the children, are provided, as are details about available records (many of the songs having been recorded).

Ginglend and Stiles are in favour of dance experiences to develop better locomotion in the children. An educational method which deals specifically with co-ordinated movement in conjunction with music has been formulated by Robins

---

1   See, also, Ward's pamphlets on the subject (1970 and 1972).

and Robins (1963). Their book offers a systematic step-by-step description of 'rhythmics' which has implications for the mental and motor development of mentally handicapped children. The authors emphasize that only persons qualified to work with the mentally handicapped should undertake to teach such co-ordinated movements; however, the method is not restricted to use by specialist instructors, it being noted that teachers who are musically or rhythmically inclined can easily adapt themselves to this teaching.

While 'rhythmics' and rhythm reading are perhaps rather different areas of interest, rhythmic movements are also a feature of the last source we shall discuss, Buker's procedure (1966) for teaching rhythm reading to intermediate educable mentally retarded children (i.e. chronological ages approximately nine to 14 years). The method is based on a structured, step-by-step programme which includes rhythm reading (quaver-, crotchet- and minim-beats, crotchet rest and repeat sign), rhythmic movements (marching, swaying, running, swinging, bending, clapping, tapping), rhythm writing and rhythm chanting. An aspect also examined is that of teacher experience and training; three teachers taught the programme, i.e. a class teacher of EMR children, a music specialist and Buker (who is himself experienced and trained both in music education and in teaching the EMR). Buker concludes that a musically untrained teacher of EMR children could, with some music aptitude, teach the programme, as alternatively a music specialist having little knowledge of the retarded.

Now that we have looked at some of the current approaches to music, we must attempt to clarify several points: firstly, the teacher's role (specialist versus non-specialist), and secondly, the question of curriculum development. These are issues to be discussed in the next chapter.

Chapter Two

The Foundation for a Project

Having looked briefly at some of the relevant literature on methods, we now have a basis to discuss the project which prompted this book. We refer to a research endeavour which we undertook in the early 1970s to explore the feasibility of classroom teachers doing music with ESN children. Our investigation centred round a one-year (32-week) field experiment based at a special school for ESN children in Cheshire. There, three full-time class teachers, all non-specialist as regards music,[1] implemented a music programme devised by the present writer. The chronological age range of the three participant classes was approximately eight to 13 years.

Obviously, the two points we raised at the end of Chapter One loom, here, as integral issues, and we shall consider these in the next paragraphs.

Rationale for our project

Our research, induced by the existing dearth of purposeful musical provision in ESN schools, originated in several considerations, namely:

1. the existing shortage of specialist music teachers at schools for the ESN (Schools Music Association report, 1964);
2. the implications in music education literature that music teachers, at least at the primary level, need not

1 In using the term 'specialist teacher' we have adopted the interpretation proposed by the National Advisory Council on the Training and Supply of Teachers (Ministry of Education, 1954, p.30).

necessarily be skilled musicians — and in this regard, the emphasis given to pedagogical skill, enthusiasm, delight in music and sense of style (e.g. Colwell, 1970; Department of Education and Science, 1969a);

3. the view frequently expressed in the literature that the class teacher is the person best placed to lead the children's music in an ESN school (e.g. Schools Music Association, 1964; Dobbs, 1966);

4. the suggestion in the Schools Music Association report, 1964, that teachers of ESN children should have some knowledge of methods in infant and junior music making;

5. the recognized value of music for the ESN child (see Chapter One); and

6. the hypothesis that musical achievement is a valid pursuit for these children (Erickson, 1970; Vernazza, 1967).

The present shortage in special schools of specialist music teachers, plus the increasing value attached to the arts in special educational literature, has prompted a need for musical information addressed specifically to the non-specialist. As Ward points out (1970), teachers proficient enough to make music invigorating for their pupils are at a premium in special schools.

Nor is this situation confined to Britain. In Erickson's survey of classroom teachers of EMR children in Colorado (1970), at least half the teachers indicated they had received no information about teaching music to the EMR child, while greatest interest was expressed for knowledge of music teaching techniques that seem to 'work' with retardates. The situation in America is such, comments Nocera (1972), that there is little likelihood of the special education teacher finding a course that will assist him to use music effectively and integrally in his work as a whole.

British teachers, it is true, can obtain some help through short courses offered by many local education authorities, advisory visits available from LEA music advisers and annual national summer courses organized by the Standing Conference for Amateur Music, but there is still a need for more information in this field in order to expand upon the practical ideas of such educators as Alvin (1965), Dobbs (1966), Nordoff and Robbins (1971) and Bailey (1973). As Lady Hamilton notes (preface to Bailey's book), we are only now evolving methods for teaching the mentally handicapped, and as yet we know little about teaching them music.

The present book endeavours to expand upon the available information, concentrating particularly on the needs of the musically inexperienced teacher. In our project, the teachers' participation was significant for two reasons: (1) they were the children's class teachers, and (2) they were non-specialist as regards music. The rationale behind this choice of participants is based on the considerations which we noted, together with supporting sources, at the beginning of this section. Since the issue of non-specialist music teaching is so crucial to our cause, we can perhaps gain a clearer perspective by examining what such sources have to say.

Colwell states, for example (1970, pp. 75—76): 'Musicians like to believe that the more musical one is, the more successful he will be as a teacher; all evidence indicates this is not so. Some of the best teachers of music are elementary classroom teachers who know more about pedagogy than about any one subject matter area. Minimums are necessary for every area of knowledge to be taught, even at the first-grade level, and knowledge above the minimum certainly adds to the potentiality for successful teaching. Beyond that, however, are factors such as interest in and commitment to teaching, personality and leadership abilities, knowledge of methods and materials. These apply to all areas of teaching including music.'

Similar views on the issue of music teaching, in this case particularly pertinent to our topic, were uncovered by a Schools Music Association survey of 167 ESN schools [1964]. According to the Association report (pp. 3—4):

'More than half the schools replied to this question [i.e. suggestions on the training and supply of music teachers], and the majority of these would welcome a trained music specialist, but regarded the essential requirement to be an enthusiastic, gifted and well-trained teacher as the most important factor, and musical ability to come second. All stressed the shortage of really well qualified staff, and many expressed the view that all teachers in ESN schools should have training in music teaching, and that all should play the piano. It was felt that knowledge of methods in Infant and Junior music making was needed, and the use of percussion extended . . .

One school advocated courses for experienced special school teachers, rather than places in special schools for trained specialist teachers, on the grounds that specialist subject teachers are rarely able to adapt, and in these schools it is of first importance to have teachers able to teach these children . . .

While some schools felt that specialist teachers were "out" as far as special schools were concerned, they wanted, as one school put it, "teachers of handicapped children given (a) much more initiation into the use of ingenious or unusual techniques in music-making, and (b) a greater chance to develop their own musical talents along less orthodox lines, instead of the stereotyped brand of music teaching which staff seem to think is expected of them".

. . . The objection of one school to a specialist teacher was that the children needed a stable classroom atmosphere and constant changes of teacher prohibits this. All this lends point to the comments of two schools — "the need for general subjects teachers with a love of music, and ability to teach it"; and "the chief need is for one or two enthusiasts who will make music as lively and enjoyable and varied as possible, understanding of the children and their particular needs being more important than a very high degree of skill in musicianship".'

In not dissimilar vein, the Department of Education and Science consider the attributes of music teachers, generally (1969a). They believe that to be a good music teacher, one must be fascinated by music and be able to vitalize it, displaying a sense of style. One will not necessarily be a knowledgeable musician or a capable instrumentalist, effectiveness being dependent rather on a combination of personality, pedagogics and musical skill, and strength in one aspect often in fact countering weakness in another. The sense of style to which they refer is said to differ only in degree from that of the professional musician, emanating from the fact that music is a linear art whose re-creation depends on a sense of rhythm, timing and emphasis. Such appreciation of style is partly inborn, but with practice, even those of modest abilities are believed capable of developing expertise.

A further point made in the same source, and which we find equally relevant, is that class teachers do most of the music teaching in primary schools, partly so music can be introduced as an integrated part of the whole curriculum, and partly to maintain continuity in the staff. This point has particular significance in the special school where, in consequence, the class teacher may be *preferred* as the person to lead the children's music. Dobbs sums up the class teacher's role, here, as follows (1966, p. 16):

'If what has been said about the basic need of the slow learner for security is valid, it follows that the person who is with him for most of the time, who shares his interests and general activities, in whom he can confide, and whose attitude is dependable and predictable is also the person who should be responsible for his music. He can relate it to the child's other activities and everyday living much more satisfactorily than a specialist who sees the group only a few times a week . . .'

It is now perhaps fairly obvious: that we embarked on our project reconciled to the above views. Music activities were prepared for the use of our three special school teachers on the assumption that, although non-specialists musically, their pedagogical skill in teaching was of primary importance and any musical proficiency or musical talent they might possess, secondary, and that as class teachers they were advantageously placed to undertake such activities with ESN children.

Aims and objectives of our project

Having outlined a rationale, we are ready to discuss purposes. The primary aims of our research were: (1) to design a music programme for ESN children which could be translated and enacted in the classroom by the classroom teacher, and (2) to provide a provisional evaluation of this programme within the constraints set up by access to schools and general resources. A further aim was (3) to explore, both generally and specifically, the achievement possibilities of ESN children who are taught music by the non-specialist teacher. In the long-term sense, it was hoped that the study of particular programming processes would clarify the sorts of problems and barriers that teachers of the ESN, generally, might have in working with the unfamiliar teaching material of music. It was also hoped that a contribution might be made to the investigation of learning milieux.

Because of the dual concerns in planning this programme, i.e accommodation of both the teachers and the pupils, a distinction was made between the deviser's objectives for the former (i.e. general teaching aims) and those for the latter (i.e. educational objectives, or objectives which would be operationalized through the teaching).

The general teaching aims were: (1) that the teachers should understand the material and method of each activity; (2) that they should be able to translate and enact it within their own teaching milieux, and (3) that they should elicit a positive response from their pupils. These were the aims which were investigated daily as the project teachers worked with the musical material.

The teaching was, however, directed towards the pupils, and so objectives at the pupil level were also a concern. Indeed, this accords with the usual course of pupil-focused curriculum planning whereby more detailed educational objectives are advocated in addition to the general aims which are the declaration of intent. Since the pioneering and influential work of Bloom, *et al.* (1956, 1964), a 'behavioural' classification has been dominant by which educational objectives are to state specifically how an individual is to act, think or feel after an instructional experience; or, in terms of the present project, how pupils are to behave as the result of musical experiences. The supporting literature makes it clear that the purpose of such objectives is to clarify the planning of curriculum, the selection of content and activities for attainment of the objectives, and the formulation of evaluation techniques for their appraisal (Tyler, 1949; Bloom, Krathwohl and Masia, 1964; Taba, 1962).

On the face of it this appears straightforward enough, but in the event we hit a number of snags.

Problems in using educational objectives in this project

Although the behavioural objectives' model is widely advocated in much curriculum theory, the approach is not without its limitations, and indeed we find that its appropriateness at a primary level in the present investigation proved questionable. To be more precise, there were doubts whether such objectives were really necessary for the use of the teachers. We list, here, the more obvious limitations:

1. the very uniqueness of classroom situations, which naturally questions whether a schedule of objectives can be operationalized consistently from teacher to teacher (Stenhouse, 1970/71);
2. the nature of our subject area, the arts, where precise

specification of objectives may not be possible, and when possible may not be desirable, in view of music's creative element (Eisner, 1967a);

3. teaching material unfamiliar to the teachers concerned, and the consequence that, as non-specialists, they may not understand specific musical objectives;

4. a disinclination of teachers, when planning courses, to use objectives in advance and precisely, and the secondary importance they tend to accord formal evaluation (Taylor, 1970; Jackson and Belford, 1965); and

5. the dynamic process of teaching, which may be hindered by, or limit the effectiveness of, objectives (Eisner, 1967a; Jackson, 1968).

In view of these possible limitations to the teachers' use of educational objectives, the behavioural objectives' approach was abandoned in our project at the teacher level. In the teachers' case it seemed more appropriate to follow the suggestions of Eisner (1969a, b) who talks of establishing directions and using *expressive* objectives; and of Stenhouse (1970/71) who talks of formulating hypotheses as to the possible *range* of effects (both positive *and* negative) of realizing a programme.

In the event, the suggestions of both educators were adopted. Before we describe our procedure, let us briefly explain 'expressive objectives'. According to Eisner (1969a): 'An expressive objective describes an educational encounter: It identifies a situation in which children are to work, a problem with which they are to cope, a task in which they are to engage; but it does not specify what from that encounter, situation, problem, or task they are to learn'. In other words, there is no attempt to pre-specify expected pupil behaviour.

Our procedure, then, was one of orientation, and *not* the definition of expected pupil attainment: beginning with the subject material, themes (or expressive objectives) were identified and described for the teachers, and hypotheses were generated regarding the possible effects of the encounters. Altogether seven expressive objectives were delineated: imitation of rhythms; rhythmical speech; melody; songs and accompaniments; improvisation; notation; and integrative topics. In planning content, we concentrated on choosing sensorimotor experiences organized within a repetitive, structured and progressively more difficult framework. The essential requirement for the teachers was to maintain musical order in each activity.

Since the presentation of our seven expressive objectives would be a rather protracted undertaking, we shall here choose just one of them in illustration:

Notation: The children explore the two aspects, rhythm and pitch, first separately and later combined. Rhythmic notation, which is introduced as an extension of the melody topic, is based on word association and a colour system; pitch notation, which is introduced much later by way of notated improvisation activities, is taught by the traditional means of the staff. Whatever is entailed in the notation work, it is always practically applied in some sort of performance. Hypotheses as to effects: this activity may stimulate the child's rhythmic sense, aural and visual perception, pitch discrimination, ability to read and write music, motor control and instrumental proficiency. On the other hand, the child may have difficulties associating sounds and symbols, translating these symbols in performance, and performing rhythm combined with pitch; or he may find the notation work generally confusing, or too involved for his powers of concentration; or he may tire of it and even become bored by it.

Where educational objectives were of use

Whilst the behavioural objectives' approach was not favoured for the teachers, it did, on the other hand, prove useful to the deviser. We refer to one particular issue, the investigation of achievement. As Taylor points out (1971), limited, behavioural objectives are justifiable when we are attempting to transmit concepts, specific information or training in a given skill. It may be recalled that one of the aims of our project was to explore, both generally and specifically, the achievement possibilities of ESN children who are taught music by the musically non-specialist teacher. Our programme activities were thus planned *partly* in terms of pre-specified achievement objectives.

Before we consider these objectives, let us first clarify one point. Since musical achievement figures as an aspect of our study, it will perhaps be realized that we view music not in a purely functional role, as is the case with strict 'music therapy' approaches, but with due regard for music's integrity as an art form and area of content. This does not mean our aim is to train ESN children as musicians, but simply that the fundamentals of musicianship need not be overlooked.

Now to the objectives. These concern the acquisition of cognitive and psychomotor skills, as itemized below. A rigidly specific formulation was not attempted, lest this result in over-simplifying matters. Nor were we concerned with a hierarchical presentation. For a more detailed breakdown of the skills, the reader is referred to the evaluation chapter.

Skills to be mastered

a. Cognitive skills
   1. The ability to identify three treble staff pitches.
   2. The ability to perceive pitch, melody, rhythm and harmony.
b. Psychomotor skills
   1. The ability to play a musical instrument (from an assortment of pitchless and pitched percussion).
   2. The ability to make a musical instrument (maracas; bongo drums).
   3. The ability to perform instrumental music: (1) re-creating (rote; reading based on rehearsal; sightreading), (2) improvising.

In two respects we have followed the example of Blyth, *et al.* (1972): in the use of the term 'skills', which they define as 'facility acquired through learning'; and in the inclusion of psychomotor elements in the skills area. This arrangement may be contrasted with Bloom, *et al.* (1956, 1964) whose taxonomy of educational objectives treats as yet only two domains, cognitive and affective — a third, psychomotor, impending. In relation to the Bloom analyses, the first two skill objectives listed above appear to have the best 'fit' under a cognitive label. The term 'psychomotor', on the other hand, is used with the meaning Colwell attaches (1970), namely that motion (activity, skills, physical accomplishment) is due to the mind and body working in interaction.

The second cognitive skill, concerning general musical abilities, was the basis for statistical evaluation in this project, data being derived from pre- and post-testing of comparison groups (i.e. the experimental group versus a group not exposed to the programme). The other skills, being relatively specific to our experimental programme, and thus to the

tryout population, appeared to be less amenable to such pre-
and post-test comparisons with an external group and
accordingly their assessment was confined to internal validity
judgements tendered within the context of an evaluation
model which we shall describe in the next section.

The evaluative tools for all our skill objectives were
deviser-constructed, though in two instances recourse was
made to available materials. The second cognitive skill, for
example, was assessed using a modified version of an existing
test, while the tool for the first psychomotor skill objective
was derived in part from the classification system developed
by Elizabeth Simpson (1966) and reproduced in Colwell's
book (1970, pp. 103–104).

The evaluative structure

Although the conventional approach to programme
evaluation was not used in this project, a brief description of
that procedure will give us a clearer perspective. The
approach we refer to derives from the experimental tradition
in educational research and involves an assessment of the
degree to which pre-specified criteria or objectives are
achieved. As Wiseman and Pidgeon explain (1970), it is one
stage in the predictive model of curriculum development, the
other stages comprising: (1) the definition of objectives in
behavioural terms, and (2) the selection and invention of
learning situations designed to achieve these objectives. The
tools for conventional evaluations are varied, but most often
stress the use of 'objective' tests and measures which will
yield quantitative data for statistical analyses.

While commonly advocated, this approach has recently
been the subject of criticism (see, e.g., Stenhouse, 1970/71;
Taylor, 1971; Parlett and Hamilton, 1972). The last-named
give a particularly lucid account of the objections, arguing
that educational situations are too complex to be elucidated
adequately through such evaluations; that the technological
approach ignores the often significant modifications that an
innovatory programme undergoes when adopted; that the
search for primarily quantitative information by objective
means can lead to neglect of other perhaps more salient data
which is disregarded as being 'subjective' or 'anecdotal', etc.;
and that innovatory programmes cannot be divorced from
their learning milieux.

In our study, the 'scientific' approach proved similarly
limited. What we required was a less simplistic design which,

whilst allowing for the assessment of achievement, would also elucidate the broader contexts associated with the programme's operation. In the event, the *illuminative evaluation* approach of Parlett and Hamilton (1972) was adopted as a model. This alternative procedure, which has overtones in anthropological and sociological research, concentrates not on the measurement of educational products, but instead on the intensive examination of the programme, itself (i.e. its rationale and evolution, operations, achievements and difficulties), emphasizing observation at the classroom level and interviews with participating teachers and pupils. In keeping with the illuminative evaluation approach, we collected data from four areas: observation, questionnaires, documentary sources and tests.

Outline of our investigation

To close the chapter, it may be useful to describe the stages of our research, since the research provides a basis for this book.

Our investigation began with a period of orientation in which the literature was surveyed, and visits were made to a number of schools for ESN children, and, for purposes of comparison, several special schools for other handicaps. These initial investigations into the specific *organization* or field situation in which our research topic was to be studied, lent support to a rationale for our project and led to a more intensive examination of the basic variables relevant in planning the music programme, i.e. the schools, the teachers and the pupils. At this stage, aims and objectives were tentatively considered and a provisional outline of the experimental programme was drawn up.

A short pilot programme was next developed, then implemented at one of the ESN schools ('Brockton' School) previously visited; in this case the teaching was done by the writer. On the basis of this trial of some of the envisaged activities of the experimental programme, further planning and development proceeded.

In the meantime sampling was begun in order to select the school, the teachers and the pupils who would be participating in the experimental situation, and in addition, a second school which would provide a contrast (control) sample of children for comparisons of test results — in the event, 'Dunbar' and 'Hudson' schools, respectively.[1] Simultaneously, some investigations into musical ability were made and a modification of the Bentley tests *Measures of Musical Abilities* (1966a), was undertaken. The modified tests, in pilot form, were run at Brockton School, the same school where the pilot programme was implemented. Test revisions were made, and a final version of the modified battery was developed. The test battery in its final form was then given to both experimental and contrast children (i.e. Dunbar and Hudson), just prior to implementation of the official programme at the experimental school, Dunbar.

Upon completion of the music testing, the one-year experimental programme involving three classroom teachers and their respective classes, was begun at the experimental school. Project objectives were reconsidered; decisions were made as to how to disclose objectives to the teachers; and the educational objectives which had been tentatively formulated for the deviser's use, were reviewed, relative to the proposed exploration of musical achievement. The main source of data for examining the research topic was viewed as the field situation during programme enactment. Evaluation centred upon continuous data collection, using techniques in keeping with the evaluation strategies of primarily qualitatively-based researches. Revisions to the programme were made throughout the period of implementation as a result of the continual analysis and interpretation of the data collected.

Upon termination of the programme, both the experimental and contrast children were retested with the same modified music tests which had been given prior to the programme. The results of these music tests on pre- and post-programme occasions were then subjected to statistical comparison and analysis.

The final examination and interpretation of all the data helped to clarify the two major issues which were implicit throughout the investigation: a curriculum theme which tried to explain the operation of a specifically devised music programme in the hands of non-specialist teachers of the ESN; and, arising out of the first, a music education theme

---

1 The term 'contrast' was selected in preference to 'control' even though the children in Hudson were chosen with care, with a view to control for probable main variables such as ESN status, age, sex and socioeconomic background. The rationale for the choice of the term 'contrast', assuming as it does the stated attributes of 'control', is that comparisons were not made between the schools across the board of variables.

which tried to discover relationships between musical approaches and the ESN child, i.e. whether particular approaches 'work'. A focusing of the investigation culminated in attempts to uncover general principles within a broader explanatory context.

There were two major developments of our research, as the reader is probably aware, i.e. the music programme and the musical ability test. These will be discussed, individually, in future chapters. First, however, we shall examine the participants who were involved in our project.

Chapter Three

The Participants

In this chapter we shall look at the schools, the teachers and the pupils who were involved in our project, and we shall confirm the typicality of our ESN population in relation to the ESN population, generally. Our discussion will thus focus on the issues specific to educational subnormality.

Schools for ESN children

Our research project was undertaken in co-operation with two day special schools for ESN children in England: an experimental sample comprising 59 boys and girls were drawn from a school in Cheshire which we have called 'Dunbar',[1] while a contrast sample of 60 boys and girls were drawn from a school in Merseyside which we have called 'Hudson'. The Hudson sample functioned primarily as a contrast for statistical comparisons with Dunbar of musical ability test results; at the same time, however, Hudson provided a useful reference for general comparison as an ESN school.

It is estimated that about one per cent of school-age children attend schools for the educationally subnormal. Clarke (1969) informs us that in 1946 there were 11,000 places at ESN schools, and in 1967 there were 47,000 places, while the waiting list between 1949 and recently has remained fairly constant at around 11,000.

Definitions of educational subnormality stress the fact of

---

1 The sample was originally 60, but was reduced to 59 shortly after the summer vacation when one pupil was sent to an approved school (now community home).

educational backwardness as a criterion for special educational treatment. We quote from the Handicapped Pupils and Special Schools Regulations, 1959: 'Educationally subnormal pupils, that is to say, pupils who, by reason of limited ability or other conditions resulting in educational retardation, require some specialised form of education wholly or partly in substitution for the education normally given in ordinary schools.' According to the Ministry of Education (1961), this includes not only the innately dull but the temporarily retarded, as also pupils who may receive their special education in ordinary schools as well as those who will attend special schools. Generally, the term is associated with children whose attainments are more than 20 per cent below the normal for their age.

In theory special schools are to provide mainly for those educationally subnormal pupils whose backwardness results from limited intellectual ability, i.e. those with IQs primarily in the range 50 to 70, but in practice (see, in particular, Cleugh, 1968), ascertainment procedures can result in a more heterogeneous population being included in ESN schools, for instance borderline cases in the IQ range 70 to 80 or even higher, whose capacity to learn may be affected mainly by conditions other than limited ability.

A review of the literature, and of ascertainment reports, establishes that the most significant advantages of ESN schools in general are smaller classes, less formal organization and more individual attention; in addition, most (and we mean, here, day schools) have less than 200 pupils and are all-age, a typical ESN school including probably five or six classes of both sexes, with an age-range of perhaps six or seven to 16. Obviously, the size of a school and the ages of its pupils will relate to the child population in the catchment area, in other words the numbers within daily travelling distance; in the largest urban authorities there may be several day special schools.

It is not always realized that no formal procedure is necessary for a child to be admitted to an ESN school, only the agreement of the parent and the local education authority. However, in order to confirm the necessity for admission, an ascertainment procedure is generally used, including normally (1) a report from the child's school which outlines the child's attainments and characteristics (the standard form for this is a 3 HP 'Report by a Head Teacher on a Backward Child'), and (2) a more detailed report by the school medical officer (usually in co-operation with an educational psychologist), giving details of a medical examination, tests of intelligence and perhaps attainment, and an assessment of social and home influences (the standard form in this case is a 2 HP 'Report on a Child Examined for a Disability of Mind'). On the basis of these examinations and reports, the School Medical Officer makes his proposal to the local education authority.

Formal ascertainment, then, depends upon the child being brought forward initially for statutory examination, but we know that such referral is not always systematic since there are so many variables operating: the commitment of the head teacher, the regularity of referral of the particular school, the provision of special school places in the area, and even the behaviour of the child (dull children with behavioural problems tend to draw attention to themselves).

As we have seen, the ascertainment procedure examines such matters as intelligence, attainments and social and emotional characteristics of the child. We have not, however, mentioned age. According to the Education Act of 1944 (and subsequently 1959 and 1967), children may be ascertained from the age of two, but this is rare before the age of five; some day ESN schools do accept five-year-olds — our contrast school, for one — though early selection is not generally easy, and seven or eight is the youngest that many children are admitted. At the other extreme, some authorities will accept pupils up to the age of thirteen or fourteen.

One final point of interest to us concerns the sex ratios in mixed ESN schools. Whilst it is common to find a disproportionately larger number of boys than girls, it is not thought that this relates simply to intelligence, but probably in some measure to the behavioural factor, a boy's problems often being manifested more obviously.

The project schools

Before we proceed further, we shall briefly explain our choice of Dunbar and Hudson as the project schools. In the initial stages of the research, the School of Education at the University of Liverpool recommended to the writer several day special schools for ESN children in and around the Merseyside area; it was considered that the head teachers of these might be agreeable to the experiment. After contact with these schools, two were selected from the shortlist as meeting the criteria of: (1) particularly co-operative headmaster, i.e. willing to allow such an experiment to be undertaken at his school; (2) both boys and girls in attendance; (3) reasonable access regarding transportation, and (4) no specialist music teacher. Of the two special schools finally selected, the choice of Dunbar for the experimental sample and Hudson for the contrast, rested upon the enthusiasm shown for the project by the former school's headmaster.

The experimental school, Dunbar, is located in a municipal borough of some 55,000 people in Cheshire. Ease of communication in the area has encouraged both industrial and residential development, so that as an Excepted District under the Education Act of 1944, the borough has delegated powers for primary, secondary, special and further education; in 1972 there were approximately 13,000 children in its 42 schools.

The contrast school, Hudson, is located in an Excepted District in Metropolitan Merseyside. Like Dunbar, the Hudson locale has benefited from its strategic communication links which have encouraged both residential and industrial development. The district comprises approximately 70,000 people, and includes some 35 schools.

We find, on inspection, that our participant schools display many of the characteristics of schools for ESN children which we described previously. Both are all-age (including children between the ages of five or six and 16) with less than 200 pupils each, and both are mixed schools with a greater proportion of boys as compared to girls. The Headmaster at Dunbar has suggested that the ratio of ascertainment in his area is usually three boys to two girls, and because of this disproportion a boy could remain on the waiting list for as long as two years; a girl, on the other hand, might be given priority to help offset the imbalance of sexes in the classes. The ascertainment procedure for transfer to both Dunbar and Hudson complies with that described previously.

As we have noted, the particular advantages of most schools for ESN children are small size and small classes, which in turn permit greater individual attention than is possible in most normal schools. In the case of our project schools, we find the total population for each is in the range 120 to 160 children, with 20 per class as the upper limit (which, incidentally, is the recommended maximum per class for ESN schools as prescribed by the Department of Education and Science). From personal observation of the

Dunbar and Hudson children, the writer concluded that these features of size in an all-age school can engender a sense of stability, both socially and emotionally — the security of successive years with the same staff, in a personalized setting. The staff at Dunbar have remarked that a child need never feel completely unfamiliar in his surroundings at promotional times, for there is always the opportunity to see any teacher for whom he/she has felt a particular attachment; such visits to former teachers have been freely encouraged by the staffs at the project schools, and indeed were observed on many occasions by the writer.

We found, during our project, that a relaxed atmosphere complemented the learning activities at both Dunbar and Hudson; tasks were presented in small stages, slowly and deliberately, with much and varied repetition. Jackson's comments (1969) about curriculum in ESN schools, generally, apply — i.e. a similar range of subjects as in normal schools, but a different method of approach and depth of study, and a slower pace of learning, the tendency being towards integration of subjects rather than separate treatments, with a likely bias towards social and domestic skills, and associated '3 Rs' work. During initial visits to the project schools, the writer was told that because of the children's limited concentration spans,the more academic subjects such as reading and arithmetic were taken in the mornings, but according to a freely arranged timetable. These lessons were supplemented by various social and domestic type activities which comprised a good deal of the children's time: domestic science, woodwork, PE, swimming, games, dancing, hymn singing, religious studies, and arts and crafts. Afternoons were often left free for sports and dancing, giving the children a necessary physical outlet to balance the mental effort, however restricted, of their mornings. Out-of-school activities were also available to the children: excursions to places of interest, parties and dances, and short holidays in Wales.

Our project classes displayed some of the common characteristics of organization mentioned by various authorities: in each class there was a wide chronological age range (between two and three years), and a wide range of IQs and mental ages (see Table 1). In addition the school populations were constantly shifting because of regular reorganizations of the type described by Cleugh (1968): at Dunbar, for instance, the pupil distributions changed twice a year, once after the Summer vacation and again after the

Easter break, these being promotional times when certain of the children were chosen to move up to a higher class and new pupils were admitted to the school; the resulting reorganization affected all six classes.

Extent of music. Prior to the experimental programme undertaken at Dunbar, the provision for music at both the project schools compared with many ESN schools of similar size. The general musical picture for ESNs can be summarized from the previously cited Schools Music Association survey of 167 ESN schools (1964), i.e. in most cases, no trained music specialist, the responsibility for music activities resting with the class teachers, themselves; in general, no systematic scheme of music teaching, typically about one hour being spent in music per class each week, and perhaps one half hour for music which is part of other lessons; on the whole, a rather stereotyped variety of activities, the most frequently pursued being song singing, hymn singing, music and move-ment, and percussion playing (using non-pitch instruments); wide use of BBC school music broadcasts, especially those involving music and movement and singing; in general, access to radio, record player, tape recorder, piano, and often pitchless percussion instruments and recorders (other in-struments, less common); and in most cases, no music room, music being taken either in the hall or the classroom or both.

We find a similar situation in our project schools prior to the experiment: i.e. no music specialist, music provision being dependent on the class teachers; no systematic scheme of music teaching; a hymn singing session held weekly and involving all pupils, plus some music and movement activities for the younger children, dancing for the older ones, occasional song singing (half an hour per week for Dunbar's Group 1), even more occasional percussion playing (more regularly for Hudson's Group 1), and the use of several BBC children's broadcasts in conjunction. Outside school hours Dunbar's Deputy Headmaster undertook a little instrumental teaching which, at the time, involved two children (including one of the experimental pupils) who were learning the recorder and the melodica, respectively. Both schools had access to a piano, a variety of percussion instruments (both pitched and pitchless), and also a radio, record player and tape recorder, the latter equipment being mainly used for music and movement, dancing and also for music listening — e.g. after dinner at Dunbar, the children were permitted to play records in the hall. In both schools the hall doubled as the dining room, and music was taken both there and in the classroom — i.e., the hall generally for hymn singing, music and movement, dancing, etc., and the classroom for most other musical activities. Upon initiation of the experimental programme, the existing musical activities continued, and as we shall see later, this had particular repercussions for Dunbar's Teacher 1.

Sampling. In order that a variety of children might be studied, it was decided that three differently-aged classes should be involved in our project (and thus, as regards the experimental school Dunbar, also three different teachers). From discussions with educators both within and without special schools, the writer concluded that children in the age range of roughly eight to 13 would probably respond most favourably to the programme: they would not be too young to cope with regular and necessarily intensive music lessons, and they would not be too old to feel really self-conscious and inhibited in their reactions. Initially, the writer discussed her programme with all the staff members at Dunbar, and since no objections to it were raised at that time, particularly to the possibility of their participation in its teaching, the Headmaster provisionally selected three teachers from the junior division of the school. This choice of teachers, while corresponding to the writer's intention to study differently-aged groups of ESN children within the stated age range, also reflected the Headmaster's design to select teachers of widely differing personalities and varying musical backgrounds (we shall say more about this later). Once the provisional choice had been made, each teacher was approached individually. All three agreed to participate provided that (1) they could terminate the lessons in the early stages if there were obvious signs of failure, and (2) they could request the writer's help if at any time difficulties should arise.

When the experiment began, there were 20 pupils in each of the three Dunbar classes, distributed in the following proportions: Group 1, 10 boys/10 girls; Group 2, 20 boys; Group 3, 11 boys/9 girls; Total, 41 boys/19 girls. However, a reorganization of the school's pupils occurred after the Summer vacation, affecting the experimental sample as follows: (1) Group 2 changed from an all-boys' class to a class of mixed sexes, (2) Group 3 lost five girls and four boys to the senior division of the school, (3) Group 1 gained seven girls from the infant's class and three boys who were new to the school, and (4) Group 2 lost one boy to an approved school (i.e. community home). These gains, losses and changes within groups necessitated some further music testing of individuals, and a compensatory attitude in the presentation of music lessons, for a certain amount of revision was required to help new pupils to familiarize themselves with their new class's previous experience of the musical activities. In the event, the Summer reorganization was the only distributional change during the experiment.

The *revised* experimental sample, numerical details of which are given in Table 1, provided a basis for the matching between Dunbar and the contrast, Hudson. Initially it was hoped to match the experimental and contrast samples by sex, age and IQ (or Mental Age) but the exact matching of schools for sex imposed constraints when matching on the other independent variables, particularly age, with the result that Hudson was significantly older than Dunbar.[1] This situation is a function of the specific schools selected and illustrates the difficulties involved in matching populations as disparate on pupil characteristics as English ESN schools, given variations in types of referral, variation in the range of problem behaviours shown by the children and differences in the overall incidence of referral to schools even within the same local authority.

The experimental teachers

During the course of our programme at Dunbar, two different teachers were assigned to Group 3 (Teacher 3a prior to the Summer vacation and Teacher 3b for the remainder of the project period). There were thus four main participants in the teaching, two male teachers and two female; in addition, both the Headmaster and the Deputy Headmaster had occasion to teach a few of the lessons during absences of the regular teachers.

As we have suggested, the main participants were of widely differing personalities and varying musical backgrounds. All were in their early 30s and had had between seven and 12 years' teaching experience:

a. *Teacher 1*, the most musically proficient of the ex-

---

1 In anticipation of matching problems, the writer gave the music tests to more Hudson children than numerically were needed.

Table 1: Sampling details

THE SCHOOLS

	Dunbar	Hudson
No. of children	120	156
No. of classes	6	8
Average nos. in classes	20	20

THE EXPERIMENTAL AND CONTRAST SAMPLES

	Dunbar	Hudson
No. of children	59	60
Initial age span (mos.)	103–161	102–170
IQ range (WISC)[1]	54–92	56–87
Boys/girls	38/21	37/23

THE GROUPS WITHIN THE SAMPLES

	Group 1		Group 2		Group 3	
	Dunbar	Hudson	Dunbar	Hudson	Dunbar	Hudson
No. of children	20	20	19	20	20	20
Initial age span (mos.)	103–127	102–135	120–144	123–153	140–162	146–170
IQ range (WISC)	58–84	59–86	56–92	57–85	54–88	56–87
Boys/girls	12/8	12/8	10/9	11/9	16/4	14/6

perimental teachers and the school pianist, suffered from an asthmatical condition which necessitated occasional absences during term and prompted a fairly low strain threshold; for various reasons to be mentioned later, this teacher was perhaps the least happy of the participants as regards the experimental teaching.

b. *Teacher 2* was the most eager to undertake the programme, regarding it as a challenge and a means to become a more interesting and competent teacher; although having had piano lessons as a child, this teacher admitted to needing much practice before feeling confident enough to play accompaniments at school.

---

1   Wechsler (1949).

c. *Teacher 3a*, while quite willing to attempt the music teaching, was very apprehensive and lacking in confidence; although fond of music, particularly singing, this teacher had no musical training apart from that received when at school, and even admitted to being 'non-musical'. After the Summer vacation, Teacher 3a took on a remedial post at Dunbar.

d. *Teacher 3b*, the new teacher assigned to Group 3 following the vacation, was reluctant though willing to undertake the music; having had no musical training apart from a brief encounter with the violin when at school, this teacher was a little self-conscious about singing and found it difficult to learn the melodies of unfamiliar songs.

We might also mention the other two, albeit transient, participants:

e. *The Headmaster* was convinced of his own lack of musical ability 'in every sense of the term', as he said, but was keen to try his hand at the lessons.

f. *The Deputy Headmaster* was also keen, so keen in fact that he expressed a desire to do music on a regular basis; his aptitude and enthusiasm found expression in a little in-strumental teaching after school hours, when, as we have already noted, he gave freely of his time to instruct one or two children in the recorder and melodica.

The ESN child

Before we take a closer look at our project pupils, we shall outline those characteristics and problems which can be associated with ESN children in general.

Clarke (1969) traces three separate aetiological popu-lations among the mildly subnormal, that is, IQs 50 to 75: (1) normal genetic, (2) pathological, which is a minority in this IQ range, and (3) subcultural. The last category is perhaps the most significant for this study since, as Clarke explains, it results from a complex genetic/environmental interaction, adverse nurturing being viewed as an important contributing feature. The category is thus probably relevant to a fair proportion of pupils in ESN schools, for a great many of these have experienced prolonged adversity: such negative environmental influences can include on the one hand, material shortcomings, such as poor standards of food, clothing, sleeping accommodation or living conditions, generally; on the other, deprivation of a higher order, such as inadequate care or supervision, defective family relationships and unstimulating verbal environment (see Douglas, 1964).

A collation of information from standard sources (Jackson, 1969; Cleugh, 1961, 1968; Tansley and Gulliford, 1965; Clarke, 1969), reveals those characteristics which can be commonly associated with ESN children at special schools, namely:

1. Slower than usual learning speed, roughly one-half to three-quarters the rate of normal children.

2. General learning difficulties: poor memory; short attention span; difficulties in grasping abstractions and forming concepts; confusion in reasoning when several ideas are presented simultaneously; poor language development (usually better on performance tests than verbal tests); difficulties in associating and systematizing experience, and hence a tendency to lack insight.

3. An indisposition to learn: motivation may have been blunted by lack of success; tendency to be less curious, to dodge difficulties and to guess wildly.

4. Emotional development slower: tendency to live for the immediate moment, to act upon the first impulse; can be gullible, easily led; generally lacking in confidence.

5. In some cases, personality disturbances — e.g. aggressiveness, withdrawal, maladjustment — which may relate to the child's learning problems, an adverse home environment, perhaps both.

6. Sometimes specific learning complaints.

7. Tendency to below par all-round fitness: overall physical development may be slower; often a greater frequency of minor physical ailments and defects (sensory defects; ear, nose and throat conditions; speech defects); there may be poor home standards — hygiene, diets, lack of adequate rest; sometimes a secondary handicap (e.g. epilepsy, haemangioma); sometimes a serious illness in infancy (e.g. hydrocephalus, meningitis).

8. Amongst subcultural subnormals, a higher proportion of dull and deficient relatives than amongst members of the normal population (Clarke, 1969).

9. Probably from three to five per cent of ESNs in special schools have brain damage (Tansley and Gulliford, 1965). According to Birch (1964), the term 'the brain-damaged child' does not necessarily refer to the brain-damaged, as such, but rather has been linked with a behaviour syndrome,

and he defines as follows those symptoms which appear frequently and variously in such children:

(a) Disordered behaviour.
(b) Short attention span.
(c) Emotional lability.
(d) Social incompetence.
(e) Defective work habits.
(f) Impulsiveness and meddlesomeness.
(g) Specific learning disorders.

An overlap with preceding traits is here obvious.

The points we have described above as being typical of many ESN pupils imply certain educational needs for this population which in turn have relevance for our programme, that is:

1. Slower teaching pace; one learning step at a time within a structured context; repetition.
2. A direct, straightforward approach.
3. The need to motivate learning.
4. The need to promote successful experiences.
5. Consideration of ways to stimulate attention.

Our experimental and contrast pupils
The characteristics which we have listed concerning ESN children generally are typified by the experimental and contrast pupils who participated in our present project. The majority, we found, came from lower working-class, poorer homes. Many had been subjected to material deficiencies and/or deprivation. Large families, i.e. five or more children, were the rule, and with it overcrowding — for example, in both samples there were several instances of seven- and eight-children families, and one family in each sample with 12 children; at least 14 of the experimental sample of 59 and 16 of the contrast sample of 60 had sisters, brothers, cousins or other relatives who were either educationally subnormal or severely subnormal; and 10 of the experimental pupils and 12 of the contrast were known to have parents one or both of whom were below average in intelligence, or who were illiterate, or who had had a psychiatric history. In both samples, there were cases of broken homes where parents had separated, one parent had deserted, a father had been sent to

prison or children had been placed in care because of deprivation or cruelty.

The incidence of minor, in some cases, major, physical disabilities was quite high amongst the sample pupils. Complaints associated with the ears, nose and throat were general, and with the respiratory system — for example, adenoidal problems, running ears and earache, tonsilitis and catarrhal conditions. Other common disabilities were enuresis (two experimental pupils, three contrast); co-ordination problems (five experimental, three contrast); sensory defects of sight and/or hearing (10 experimental, 12 contrast) ; and speech defects (five experimental, six contrast). For a number of the project pupils, disabilities necessitated hospitalization, for example in the following Dunbar cases: severe burns, cerebral thrombosis, epilepsy, heart ailment (hole-in-the-heart surgery), haemangioma of arm, hydrocephalus, meningitis, osteomyelitis, poliomyelitis, pneumonia and pyloric stenosis. The contrast sample included children with similar complaints: right hemiplegia, hydrocephalus, otitis, dislocated hip, poliomyelitis, meningitis and epilepsy.

A general lack of fitness was often seen due to insufficient sleep. There were continual instances of sample children who kept late hours, usually, said their teachers, because of watching television, but in some cases because of poor sleeping accommodation due to overcrowding, and disturbances created by the youngest members of a large family.

Unwise feeding was another common problem; for some children the provision of milk and hot dinners at school was apparently the only real nourishment they received in the day.

Lastly, both samples included children with various personality disturbances — aggressiveness (eight experimental pupils, seven contrast), withdrawal (three children in each sample), maladjustment (five experimental pupils, four contrast), and in two instances delinquency (a boy from each sample having appeared in juvenile court).

Now that we have looked at the participants who were involved in our project, we shall consider, in the next chapter, one of the major developments of the research, i.e. our music programme.

Chapter Four

The Programme

We have now discussed several points directly relevant to the planning of our programme: our participants; some of the current approaches to music with ESN children; and musical objectives. It has been noted, too, how we have viewed music not in a purely functional role (where, for instance, activities might be planned to achieve various non-musical objectives), but rather with due regard for music's integrity as an art form and area of content. Indeed, we have presupposed that music is of value to the ESN child, and have concentrated on the subject material of music itself, in other words on what we can do, given our project's variables. In the paragraphs to follow we shall consider our subject material in some detail, looking first at the basis of our programme and then its dimensions.[1]

Key concepts

An initial step in our planning was the use of basic ideas or concepts, a procedure adopted from the models of Taba (1962) and Blyth *et al.* (1972). For Taba, this is an essential step in selecting content, for the basic ideas about a subject represent the *fundamentals* of that discipline. Similarly Blyth *et al.*, commenting on the importance to children's understanding of concept learning over factual learning, advise that once a theme has been chosen, we should actively apply certain key concepts in selecting and treating the material within it.

In considering the basic ideas we would apply in our programme, the problem arose of how to relate these ideas to

---

1 This chapter explores the background to our programme. The programme, itself, is presented in Appendix A.

the developmental thought levels of the particular pupils. Piaget's theories, viewed in relation to music, were found to be relevant here. Going on Piaget, the ESN children in our study, aged as they were from approximately eight to 13 years (CA), were likely to be either in a pre-operational phase of mental development (having progressed through Piaget's sensorimotor period, and reached either the preconceptual or intuitive stage of pre-operational thought), or in an operational phase (having reached Piaget's penultimate stage of mental development, that of concrete operations). It is generally accepted that ESN children do not normally reach Piaget's final stage of development, that of formal operations.

According to Schmitt (1971), children at a pre-operational stage will identify with music most readily through action and manipulation, through feeling rhythm, tonal movement and metre in their bodies. With the stage of concrete operations comes a gradual organization by the child of things and events in his environment, but as Schmitt points out, in mutually exclusive classification systems such that learning situations are best planned which use just one grouping system at a time. As regards the aspect of 'conservation', intrinsic to Piaget's theories, Sergeant (1969) points to the considerable research evidence indicating that many normal children have achieved conservation of pitch by the seventh year. In addition, the tests of Pflederer (1964) concerning the conservation of tonal and rhythmic patterns, and metre, in normal children, indicate that by the age of eight many children have reached an intermediate stage of conservation, and some are approaching absolute conservation.

The above course suggested a number of basic ideas to be incorporated in our programme: rhythm, melody, sound, texture, harmony, manipulation (playing instruments) and notation. These are the focusing ideas which guided the formulation of activities.

Programme content centres around instrumental activity, usually in conjunction with singing, or with some other means of vocalization such as rhythmic chanting. The dimensions, however, are far-ranging, including song accompaniments, instrumental pieces, rhythmical work, improvisation, elementary notation, sightreading, composition, instrument-making, art work based on the songs, handwork connected with notation, pitch notation 'quizzes', musical illustrations of stories and written work about the music.

As we noted earlier, the emphasis is on sensorimotor experiences organized within a repetitive, structured and progressively more difficult framework.[1] Thus, melody and rhythmical activities are basic to the programme and provide a foundation of experience for the more challenging under-takings — instrumental work, elementary notation, impro-visation and composition. A strong interrelation exists be-tween all the programme activities, which are structured along definite developmental lines: notation is introduced through borrowings from rhythmical topics and melody; on the other hand, some rhythmic activities draw from notation topics; improvisation is based on both rhythmic work and notation, and is the prelude to composition endeavours; instrumental activity plays a prominent role in all the pro-grammed topics and ties together the areas of concern in yet another way; and a further link is provided by a number of integrative themes.

An outlines of the programme appears in Figure 1.

A closer look at the programme activities. *Basic sequences*

Rhythm. Work on the programme's design began with a consideration of topics related to the musical elements of rhythm and melody. *Rhythm* was thought to be an approp-riate starting-point because it is one of the most fundamental elements of music which affects man, a 'rhythmic' being himself. While the idea that a sense of rhythm is strongly inherent has been challenged by Hickman (1968), none-theless most of us are attracted by musical rhythm and can relate to it easily.

Goldstein and Seigle (*n.d.*) comment that rhythmical activities are basic to the music programme for educable mentally handicapped children and one of the most impor-tant aspects, while teachers surveyed in McLaughlin's study (1963) consider motor forms of learning to be particularly relevant to EMR children. Here, too, we are interested in Carlson and Ginglend's advice (1961), that a child must have an understanding of rhythm through considerable experience in clapping and tapping in time to music, before he can try more organized activities such as playing rhythmic in-struments.

In formulating the rhythmical activities for our project, we were very much concerned with two ideas, namely rhythmic

---

1   The importance of a graduated programme for retardates, now recognized by most educators, has been given impetus by researchers such as Zeaman and House (1963).

Figure 1: The programme activities and their relative importance in per cent.

A. Basic Sequences (5%)
  (a) Rhythmical activities
    1. Imitation of rhythms
    2. Rhythmical speech

B. Introduction to Notation (40%)
  (a) Rhythmic notation
    1. Introduction to ♩
    2. Handwork – ♩
    3. Word-sequences plus ♩
    4. Handwork – ♪
    5. Introduction to ♫
    6. Handwork – ♫
    7. Word-sequences plus ♫
    8. Handwork – ♫
    9. Combining ♩ and ♫
    10. a) Rhythmic imitation with
        pulse group on drums
      b) Rhythmical speech with
        pulse group on drums

  (b) Melody

  (b) Pitch notation
    1. Introduction to ♫
    2. Rhythmic imitation/
      improvisation
    3. Improvisation/notation
    4. (a) Melody topic notated (♫)
       (b) Melody topic notated (♩)
    5. Staff notation of g'
    6. Staff notation of a'
    7. Staff notation of e'
    8. Sightreading tunes based on
      the notes g' and a'; and g' and e'
    9. Staff notation of b'
    10. Sightreading tunes based on
       the notes g', a', b'; and g', e', a'
    11. Pitch notation quiz
    12. Introduction to ♩
    13. Improvisation/notation – staff
    14. Instrumental pieces

Improvisation
and composition
activities
(letter-name
notation)

Staff
notation

C. Songs and Accompaniments (40%)
(Learned by rote, apart from the occasional notated instrumental parts introduced late in the programme)

D. Extended Works (10%)
(Learned by rote)

E. Integrative Topics (5%)
  1. Instrument-making
    a) Bongo drums
    b) Maracas
  2. Art work based on the lessons
  3. Musical illustrations
  4. Exploration of sound
  5. Written work about the lessons (questionnaire)

imitation, together with verbalization. We found support for our approach in the literature: e.g. in Alvin's rhythmical activity with severely subnormal Japanese children (1971); Dobbs's methods of rhythmical patterning (1966; see also Ward, 1972); Bailey's system for teaching rhythm to severely subnormals (1973); and Winters' methods for acquiring a vocabulary of rhythmic patterns (1967a). The two activities we eventually defined for our programme, imitation of rhythms and rhythmical speech, can be examined in Appendix A, part one.

Melody. For this, the second element basic to our planning, one topic was defined in the experimental teaching. This was designed primarily to acquaint the class with the pitched percussion instruments. We were concerned with simplicity in our approach, using repeated tones or a repeated sequence of tones, and we found, like Dobbs (1966), that chime bars could be particularly useful. In our programme activity the idea of an instrumental cuckoo call using the chime bars G and E is explored, with words being set to the 2-note tune in order to provide a reference for starting and finishing, and to add interest. The words might be nursery rhymes or similar verses, perhaps invented to correspond to class interests: for example, for Group 2, which was initially an all boys' class, a car name rhyme was used, while for Group 3, we used a sequence of children's names, and for Group 1, the traditional 'Tinker, tailor . . . .' rhyme.

In this topic the children are sometimes divided, some to sing the tune, some to play it. Also, individuals are encouraged to play the tune 'solo' while the rest of the class sing and/or accompany by clapping or beating the pulse. Specific details are given in Appendix A, part one.

Lines of development: music reading. Although we can find references which discount attempts to teach notation to ESN children (e.g. McLaughlin, 1963, who on the basis of teacher surveys, rejects music reading as a suitable activity), there are other sources which actually encourage the teaching of notation. We learn from the Department of Education and Science (1969a) that both rhythm reading and pitch reading can be taught to at least some of these pupils. Alvin (1965) believes that while most subnormal children cannot progress farther than a rudimentary level of music reading, any achievement in 'reading' (or the interpretation of the written symbol) is important to a child's social status. Dobbs (1966) takes the view that we owe it to our slow-learners to help them at some stage to read simple tunes. And we have already mentioned Buker's programme (1966) for teaching rhythm reading to intermediate educable mentally retarded children.

In the present programme, music reading was viewed as a serious and worthwhile undertaking for ESN children. We describe the details of our approach in the next section.

Introduction to notation

Two aspects are considered, rhythm and pitch. The first is introduced fairly early in the programme as an extension of the melody topic; pitch is introduced much later, by way of improvisation/composition activities.

Rhythmic notation. Musical notes removed from the context of the staff are linear symbols of sounds which relate to each other in mathematical ratios (2:1 in the case of crotchets and minims, 4:1 in the case of quavers and minims, etc.). In purely mathematical terms such concepts could be difficult to teach to backward children, but the problem is greatly reduced by the adoption of two procedures: (1) word association, and (2) a colour system. These approaches would agree with O'Connor and Hermelin's findings in respect of the severely subnormal (1963), namely, that verbal coding should be a part of the task, and that the dimensions of variability between stimuli should be increased.

The theory that verbalization is important to learning has been examined in many studies (e.g. Clarke, 1969), and has been practically applied to musical rhythm learning by various educators, the most well-known of whom is probably Carl Orff. The rhythmic notation activities in our project stress verbalization, using concrete incentives at once familiar to the children — their own names. These, like any other words, are composed of syllables which can be associated with musical notes in one-to-one correspondences. Word groupings then define musical rhythms: for example, a one-syllable name such as 'John' corresponds to ♩ ; a two-syllable name such as 'Lin-da' corresponds to ♫ ; these names grouped as 'Lin-da John' define the musical rhythm ♫ ♩ The method can be extended further: 'Jen-ni-fer' ♫♩), 'Mar-i-anne' (♫♩), 'Grant O'Hare' (♩♫♩), etc. Consistency is maintained by associating a whole word with every note-block (or joined series of notes). (Here, ♩ is considered to be a note-block.) In each of our experimental classes, the names chosen to illustrate ♩ and ♫ (e.g. in Group 2, 'Frank' and 'Jimmie') were retained in subsequent notation activities as verbal labels for the symbols. To enable frequent presentations of material within a limited experimental time, the writer's lessons concentrated on introducing ♩, its binary equivalent ♫ , and the minim ♩ (which is presented in the project as ♩ ♩); these were sufficient to allow many varied activities.[1]

A heightened visual stimulus results if the rhythmic notation is also coloured. Any colours can be chosen, but a systematic approach which associates the same colour with the same note-block is preferable — in our project, crotchets were always red and quavers, blue.

Eleven rhythmic notation activities were devised for the programme (see Appendix A, part two): introduction to ♩ ; writing ♩ ; word-sequences plus ♩ ; writing ♩ ♩ ♩ ♩ ; introduction to ♫ ; writing ♫ ; word-sequences plus ♫ ; writing ♫ ♫ ♫ ♫ ; combining ♩ and ♫ ; rhythmic imitation with pulse group on drums; and rhythmical speech with pulse group on drums — the last two activities being related to the crotchet. The minim is presented at a later stage in the programme.

Pitch notation. It is often advised by music educators that practical exploration should precede theory. So, too, the dryness of mechanical exercises must be avoided. In our programme lessons a great deal of instrumental activity is incorporated before the subject of pitch notation is even introduced. The child's rote involvement with song accompaniments, improvisation and composition is stressed, these topics in turn giving him an incentive to see his own part or own 'composition' written on the staff, as a permanent record. He then has a concrete and evident reason for learning pitch notation which could motivate him to attend to the task.

---

1 The above method of presenting the 2-beat note was personally suggested to the writer by the late P.F.C. Bailey. See also, Bailey (1973).
   Because of the project's emphasis on instrumental activity, keyboard notation rather than vocal notation was adopted throughout.

The naming of pitch sounds can be important to the child's understanding of music, giving specificness to the perception. In terms of pitch perception learning, Sergeant (1969) notes that auditory sensation alone is inadequate as a stimulus and that the cognition of music depends upon equivalent visual, verbal, motor and other learning. During our project, four different pitches in various combinations were learned by the three experimental classes. Group 2 explored the notes g', a' and b', a combination which offers melodic possibilities since many simple tunes, including much recorder music, employ these three notes.[1] Group 3 explored g', e' and a', a combination which offers pentatonic possibilities; pentatonic music, being based on a five-note scale which results after eliminating the fourth and seventh degrees from the eight-note 'doh' scale, incorporates no dissonant elements and therefore is well-suited to ad lib accompaniments and improvisation. Group 1, owing to fewer lessons, managed to explore only two notes, g' and e'.

It was explained earlier that rhythmic notation is taught in our programme through word-association, colour and symbol combined. Pitch notation, on the other hand, is taught through symbol alone, i.e. the staff, a visual tool with lines, spaces and clef which operate in systematic ways. The introduction of staff notation is based on the assumption that rhythm should be thoroughly explored before pitch is attempted, thereby encouraging a clearly understood distinction between rhythm and pitch, i.e. between coloured note-symbol and its position on the staff. Regarding this point Christ (1953) has shown that the mastery of rhythm reading is the primary solution to most music reading difficulties.

Fourteen pitch notation topics were devised for the experimental programme, tracing a line of development from (a) improvisation and composition activities, which employ a letter-name method of notation, to (b) the introduction of staff notation. We must agree with Winters (1967a) that the essence of improvisation lies in the use of a framework specifying certain limits to the performance — for instance, suggestions as to length, or range of notes or harmony, etc. Ward (1970) provides a simple example of such a framework in his timbre activity: a variety of instruments are distributed

---

1   The method of letter-naming used here is that of Helmholtz (1895), pp. 15—16. See under 'Pitch', section 7(a) in SCHOLES (1970), *The Oxford Companion to Music.*

amongst the children, the teacher begins to count steadily and the children are invited to play their instruments on particular numbers.

The improvisation activities in our programme are based on the rhythmic formula ♪♪ ♩ and three pre-selected notes played within a counting framework (as per Ward); the notes are preferably set up on instruments with removable bars.

During the project, early improvisation attempts were notated by copying down the engraved letter-names from the particular bars struck on the instrument. Words were then invented for each 'composition'.

After several further activities exploring letter-name notation — this time based on the earlier melody topic — the experimental pupils were introduced to staff notation. Four different pitches, g', a', e', and b' were successively presented, sightreading topics and pitch notation quizzes were attempted and the minim beat was introduced. Further improvisational work was notated on the staff and a beginning was made on the reading of instrumental pieces.

This particular area of concern required an extensive preparation of music apparatus and materials by the writer, including many written charts. For further details, see Appendix A, part two.

Songs and accompaniments

Without doubt, song singing is the most common musical endeavour undertaken with retardates. We have already looked at the Schools Music Association report on ESN schools (1964). And in both Carey's and McLaughlin's surveys (1958 and 1963, respectively), singing was found to be the main musical activity for EMR children. The appeal of songs, which perhaps stems from their *relatively* easy assimilation, does not fully explain their importance for our children. As Carlson and Ginglend suggest (1961), songs are not just music to a retarded child but a means of expression whereby he can vocalize and express moods without having to form thoughts of his own. Moreover, songs can play a significant role in teaching language skills, as, for instance, Bereiter and Engelmann (1966) have demonstrated. With regard to singing, we can rest assured that ESN children have the potential to sing as naturally and as pleasantly as normal children, barring disorders of the vocal organs.

From the various sources which state criteria for selecting

songs for the subnormal child, the following points of advice are typical and were kept in mind in planning the present programme:[1]

1. The lines of verses should not be too long, nor should one overdo the number of verses.
2. Simple, straightforward words are needed, those standing for clear concepts; repetitiveness helps.
3. The melody should fall within the children's vocal range (we must add that this range is not always as high as many children's songs would have us believe — a comfortable range for the class should therefore be determined).
4. The harmonies should not be dull, but rather can add colour; likewise, the rhythm should be easily assimilated yet interesting.
5. The subjects of the songs should relate to the children's experiences, covering the whole range of moods, and appropriate for the children's chronological age.

Nordoff and Robbins have given particular attention to this topic in their writings (1965, 1971a, 1971b) and have, themselves, composed numerous works especially for handicapped children (see 1971b). Some of their works, characterized by a vital use of dissonance, were used in the present programme.

Undoubtedly the singing voice is preferable to the piano for teaching songs. We found, like Dobbs (1966), that vocal patterning is possible by more teachers than one might expect. Dobbs suggests three basic requirements: a repertoire of appropriate songs, a confident use of one's voice, and the ability to vitalize the material. We agree in principle. But whilst we neither expected nor wished our project teachers to have professionally trained voices, there were those amongst them who could *not* sing with confidence. To overcome this, our song teaching method relied not on the voice by itself, but rather in conjunction with a taped accompaniment (specifically, a piano version of each song, which was designed to provide each teacher, firstly, with an instrument to *support* her voice, and secondly, with a means of teaching the song by breaking it down into easily assimilated, repetitive steps. More will be said about this later).

---

1   For more information, see Dobbs (1966), Goldstein and Seigle (*n.d.*), Nordoff and Robbins (1965).

There are several advantages in the use of taped accompaniments, namely:

1. They enable the teacher's direct participation in the learning-teaching situation, allowing a greater measure of involvement than is possible if, for instance, the lesson were conducted from an upright piano.

2. Taped accompaniments obviate any need for the teacher personally to provide supporting harmonies for the singing, and thus are useful for those who do not play an instrument, yet feel the need of an instrumental support.

3. The provision of such accompaniments is equally applicable to taping from records, so that in a less hurried context teachers can do their own preparation.

One further point might be mentioned, the fact that complete scores (i.e. vocal line plus piano accompaniment) were given to our teachers for reference. Although in some instances the teachers' knowledge of notation was minimal and the score, itself, meant little to them, the full song arrangement was written out rather than just the words and melody because it was felt that visual familiarity would aid aural awareness and thus help in the teaching situation.

Amongst our three experimental classes 25 different songs were taught (by rote) using the means described. The songs included traditional songs, folk songs (English, American, Austrian, French, German), a sea shanty, carols (Czechoslovakian, English), a vocal arrangement of a keyboard piece and several songs especially composed for slow learners, or for children in general. Two of the folk songs were sung in the original languages of French and German (see the complete list in Appendix C).

Singing plus instruments. Although during our project, a fair amount of time was devoted to singing, this was never viewed as an isolated activity. In fact, the main purpose of the songs was to provide a vehicle for instrumental work, the principal content item within the programme. Most of our topics are related to instrumental activity in some way.

Support for such extensive use of instruments is readily found in the literature, but indeed our own study leaves little doubt about the value of this activity. Like Nordoff and Robbins (1971b) we realized that group music-making affords the opportunity for mutual participation in a constructive activity. And we agreed with Alvin (1965) that playing an instrument makes greater mental demands than singing, and is a more tangible enterprise since it consists in technical accomplishment. Certainly, there is a complex interplay of faculties involved: the psychomotor, the aural, the tactile and the visual. But equally important are the possible concomitant effects — the mental stimulation; the interest aroused, which can motivate a greater alertness and improved concentration; and the satisfaction gained from attainment.

The instruments which we used in our project comprised a variety of pitched and pitchless percussion instruments such as drums, triangles, tambourine, cymbal, Glockenspiel, xylophone, chime bars, etc. For each of the programme songs, the writer devised several different accompaniments which could be played on these instruments, then detailed the information on work cards for the teachers' use in teaching the children. In this, effort was made to be as explicit as possible to accommodate the non-specialist, and thus information on 'how to play' and 'when to play' was always given in relation to song texts.[1] For example, an accompaniment for *Boney was a Warrior* was explained as follows:

1. Two children, a drum each, to beat once on each syllable of the chorus, i.e. on each syllable of 'Way-ay-yah' and of 'John France-wah'.
2. One child to strike the cymbal on the accented syllables of the chorus, i.e. on 'yah' and on 'wah'.
3. One child to play the notes c" and a' on the soprano Glockenspiel, as follows:

John France-wah
c"   c"   a'

The procedure that Levin and Levin (1972) describe for instrumental activity with the severely retarded shows considerable overlap with the present programme: the use of simple classroom instruments; explaining to the child his specific responsibility in the piece; the insertion of his part in several places in the music; then cueing him when to perform.

---

1 The writer has found that editors who provide accompaniment suggestions in their song publications generally tend to assume some harmonic knowledge on the part of the teacher.

With such instruments and method, no sophisticated techniques of performance are involved, nor is there a need for the child to read music.

The techniques involved in devising song accompaniments are discussed in Appendix A, part three. Two kinds of accompaniments were attempted during our project, those for pitched percussion and those for pitchless. The latter instruments were used in several ways: as a pulse; for patterning word rhythms; for highlighting particular words; and for exploring different instrumental sounds. The pitched percussion were used as follows: as a pulse; for melodic patterning of particular words and phrases; for simplified melodies; and for pentatonic improvisation. Further information in the Appendix concerns such aspects as tuning, key knowledge and instrumental techniques, e.g. the preparation, handling and playing of the instruments, and their matching to the children.

The piano accompaniments which we taped for the song teaching provided the supporting music to which the children played during the music sessions. We arranged these supporting accompaniments from various musical sources, and thus we included omissions, additions and changes in notes as we felt were necessary to accommodate the programme. In the taping (the writer was the pianist) two points were heeded, namely that (1) each song support should include an introduction, and (2) each arrangement should be fairly full and continuous. These criteria were specified in order to create adequate aural references for the children and teachers; indeed, a taping of the few basic chords in a song such as might be strummed on the guitar or autoharp would be difficult to relate to (and to record) without the voice being taped simultaneously.

The possibilities of using other supporting music, for instance records or an instrument played by the teacher, are also considered in Appendix A.

Extended works

The enthusiasm and willingness of Teacher 2 to undergo further pressures as regards lesson preparation, encouraged us to introduce in the project two major works, *Fun for Four Drums* and *The Three Bears*, both compositions by Paul Nordoff and Clive Robbins (see Appendix B). In each case the 'breaking-it-down' technique of our song-teaching method was used and the supporting music presented on tape.

Fun for Four Drums (1968) is a musical game, learned by rote, designed to develop both concentration in listening, and some basic mastery of rhythmic control. Four different rhythms (one for each drum) are introduced in the work; appropriately, these comprise crotchet and quaver beats and so are readily learned as an extension of our programme's rhythmic notation topics: rhythm 1 = ♩ ; rhythm 2 = ♩ ♩ ; rhythm 3 = ♫ ♩ ; rhythm 4 = ♩ ♫ ♩ . Each drum part (i.e. each rhythm) has its own particular style of piano accompaniment associated with it, which soon becomes a musical cue to the children. In taping the accompaniment, we left appropriate periods of silence for the drum soloists to 'fill in' their parts; and, as with our songs, we edited the piano arrangement in order to create adequate aural references for the children and teachers. When the music had been thoroughly learned, the singers were given the opportunity to clap with the drummers; this was eventually extended to include four different clapping groups to match the four different soloists.

The Three Bears (1966) is a work designed to give creative experiences in using musical instruments. Lasting 25 minutes, it is learned by rote and contains songs, rhythmical speech, a narrative and instrumental parts for 16 children who play on cue and in specified rhythms. A variety of instruments are required — strings, simple wind instruments and percussion. At Dunbar, we adapted to the work those instruments which were available to the teacher.

Since the composers recommend that the various sections of *The Three Bears* be worked on in a specific order other than chronological, we prepared two tapes, one for rehearsals and one for the finished version. The taping involved both the piano accompaniment and the narrative. In some places we left appropriate periods of silence for the soloists to 'fill in' their parts; in others, we doubled the solo parts in the piano accompaniment. And to aid the children's entries, we added, as before, our own introductions and musical cues where they were thought to be relevant.

Integrative topics

The interest expressed by various educators in relating music to other subjects has influenced our project to a small extent. Handwork activities connected with notation have already been mentioned. Other topics were also attempted, namely, instrument-making, art work based on the songs, musical illustrations of stories, exploration of sound, and written work about the music lessons.

Instrument-making. Several sources in the literature include this activity in their programmes for the retarded, for instance Carlson and Ginglend (1961), Connor and Talbot (1964). The last-named writers mention a variety of pupil-made instruments: drums and drumsticks, rhythm sticks, harness bells, hand bells and tambourines. We were interested in the opportunities this activity affords for working with one's hands, and for stimulating a personal interest in the instrument and in playing it. Instrument-making in our project was limited to two instruments, bongo drums and maracas, both of which were used by the children in their song accompaniments. Construction details can be found in books on instrument-making (see, for instance, Blocksidge, 1957).

Art work. For the art activity, the children drew or painted pictures about the songs they were learning. In some cases a story was developed first; in others, particular aspects of a song were selected for illustration.

The classes also made and decorated music folders in which to store their handwork (i.e. notation) exercises.

Musical illustrations. It has been pointed out that music can be effective in promoting slow-learning children's awareness of the world around them. Ward (1970), for instance, notes that even the most severely subnormal children can distinguish between the sounds of our classroom instruments. For the programme, we were particularly interested in two 'sound' activities — exploration of sound (see below) and musical enrichment of stories.

The musical illustrations attempted in our project were based on stories with which the children were already familiar or which developed from the songs they were learning. It was left very much to the teacher to prompt and inspire ideas in the class. From an initial experimenting with a few sound effects, the topic developed to the point where it was possible to illustrate a whole story quite elaborately.

For example, for the children in Group 3 part of one lesson was devoted to illustrating a story about the British Grenadiers, one of their songs. With the teacher's help and prompting, a narrative was worked out and instruments introduced to illustrate various personages and events (e.g., drum and cymbal = Grenadier soldier; triangle = 4 chimes on awaking; shaking tambourine = nervousness at getting up; all the instruments at random = the assembling troops; all the instruments rhythmically = marching into battle; and a gradual acceleration and crescendo by the players = the charge, and finally the clash of arms). Once the story was certain, one of the children was helped to narrate it while the rest of the class played the instruments.

Exploration of sound. For this, the children tried to identify various sounds (sources unseen while being produced) and also to make their own. Common objects were used (jars, flower pots and copper piping struck with a nail, etc., wood blocks and sandpaper, elastic band stretched over a glass jar), as well as some of the instruments the children normally played.

Written work about the lessons. This concerns a question-naire which we devised for our pupils. For further details, see Chapter Six and Appendix G.

Operation of the programme

Our field experiment at Dunbar School was carried out over a 32-week period, beginning on the 1st of June of the school year and continuing, with a break for the Summer vacation, until Easter of the following school year. Our participant teachers, being non-specialist and of varying musical ability and training, were taxed as to their flexibility not only to interpret instruction notes prepared by an outsider — the present writer — but also to translate these into the practical situation of the classroom. The absolute minimum of preparation was allowed the teachers, generally 1–2 days per lesson, in later stages only so much as a quick read-through of the lesson plan; and most of the time they were dealing with generally unfamiliar material. The writer assumed, like Dobbs (1966), that the teachers could learn *along with* the children.

Pressures of programming within a necessarily trial-and-error research project demanded that such an approach be adopted. To enable the exploration of as many varied activities as possible within the time allotted, lessons were intensive: three sessions per week per teacher were scheduled. (We will discuss later how one teacher found the strain too much, and was forced to reduce the number of lessons taught.) The writer prepared both the lessons and the music materials, conditions of time making it impractical to rely upon teacher help in the latter regard.[1] Lesson notes were very detailed at first, it being anticipated that the teachers would then need explicit suggestions as to procedures. As proficiency amongst the teachers grew, however, it was possible to give just the barest essentials in writing, accompanied by verbal explanation if needed. The writer attended each music session as an observer, and on the basis of what she saw and heard tried to determine the suitability or unsuitability of lesson-matter, and consequently what amendments were necessary.

Although ideally music-making should be a part of school life, not restricted solely to timetabled periods but used as an integrating medium that can also enhance other learning situations, project conditions precluded such freedom at the experimental school. In order to assess day-to-day responses with continuity, a fairly strict lesson schedule was necessary. Mornings were chosen for the experimental sessions since class units were maintained then, whereas scattering occurred in the afternoons when pupils from various classes were grouped for sport and craft activities. It was intended to restrict the music lessons to twenty minutes each, but this time limit was rarely achieved because the time devoted to preliminaries, as well as practical problems encountered in the actual teaching and interruptions of one sort or another, invariably extended the sessions to 30 or 35 minutes, and sometimes, when the eagerness of teacher and class could not be contained, even upwards of an hour — this, in fact, was a frequent occurrence in Group 2. Extra sessions were arranged for all groups prior to concerts at Christmas and Easter.

Of the three lessons per week scheduled for each teacher, two sessions were concerned primarily with music, while the third was devoted to more integrative activities. This arrangement corresponded nicely with the school's curriculum: cookery and swimming instruction resulted in partial classes being present for at least one of the scheduled music periods of each group, so this particular time was chosen to do the third lesson. Other matters had to be taken into account during morning sessions — for example, weekly visits by the

---

1 Teacher 2, we might note, preferred to be involved, and actually did help with some of the materials.

pupils to the school nurse and to the school library, and monitoring jobs such as setting-up chairs in the hall for dinner. These were all part of the school's functioning and had to be accepted as such even if it meant that children were called away during class time.

The instruments

The instruments used for the experimental programme at Dunbar comprised a number of melodic and rhythmic percussion supplied by the County Council (specifically, a soprano 13-note diatonic Glockenspiel, with removable bars; an alto 13-note diatonic xylophone, with removable bars; five chime bars, c', d', e', g' and a'; one 10-inch tambourine; and one 11-inch solo cymbal), plus a collection of instruments already in the school's possession, some of poor quality, but nonetheless appreciated (specifically, a soprano 20-note chromatic Glockenspiel set in a wooden box, bars not removable; an alto 12-note diatonic Glockenspiel, bars not removable; six small drums, some with straps; seven small tambourines; an assortment of hand cymbals [Indian bells] and triangles; and two descant recorders). The children's handmade instruments included 16 drums and three sets of maracas, and on loan for the project were two soprano melodicas, another descant recorder and three dulcimers (2-string, 10-string and 25-string, respectively).

The music materials

As we noted before, the writer prepared both the lessons and the music materials for the teachers. The latter preparation involved several steps:

1. All the songs were copied out in piano-vocal arrangements (i.e. vocal line plus piano accompaniment) and made available to the teachers for reference.

2. From each song arrangement the piano accompaniment (with the notes of the vocal line incorporated) was recorded on tape, for subsequent use in class. This was done in easy stages — phrase-by-phrase or section-by-section — each fragment repeated several times, with a count-in preceding. For example, a song with two 4-bar sections was recorded as follows:

a. Each 2-bar phrase 3x, with a 4-beat count-in before each playing.

b. Each 4-bar section 4x, with a 4-beat count-in before each playing.

c. The whole accompaniment 7x, with a 4-beat count-in before each playing.

By this procedure, the teacher had both an instrumental support, and a technique for teaching the song which involved a step-by-step breakdown of the material. A similar procedure (but on a larger scale) was used to present the two extended works of the programme.

3. Work cards were devised for each song to give the teachers details of accompaniments which the children might play. We explained earlier that in order to be as explicit as possible, all such performance instructions were given in relation to song texts.

4. For notation and sightreading topics, extra large example sheets and charts were prepared to enable class viewing. The large-size scoring was also adopted when the children notated their own 'compositions'; in this case the sheets were partially prepared for them beforehand, with noteheads for letter-name notation, or lines and treble clef for staff notation.

In this chapter, we have looked at the background to our programme, hopefully to shed some light on the programme itself, as presented in Appendix A. In the next chapter, we shall consider the second major development of our research, i.e. the musical ability test.

Chapter Five

The Musical Ability Test

Just as the modern maths curriculum aims to increase the child's conceptual ability in the field of mathematics, and is not merely limited to expertise with the *contents* of problems, and literacy programmes aim to educate for skill in social sensitivity, empathy and communication, and not merely for insight into a *particular* verbal product, so the present programme aims to extend the general musical abilities of the children, a goal at a rather higher level than the acquisition of our more specific skills such as, for instance, making a drum, however valuable this might be for a given child, particularly an ESN one.[1]

In the course of our field experiment, we attempted to evaluate the success of our curriculum in extending general musical abilities, by comparing programme (i.e. experimental) and non-programme (i.e. contrast) groups of children. What we required was a test which allowed the possibility of the detection of change brought about through the programme, and correlatively, a sensitivity to the possibility of no change in the absence of the programme and which could, by that token, serve as a measure of achievement. Clearly, there must be empirical support for categorizing our test in this way. It must be more than a measure of *capacity* which, by Drever's definition (1964), denotes 'native potentiality generally, or in respect of any function'. On the other hand it might well be classed as an *ability* test if we accept Lehman's definition of musical ability (1968): 'The term "musical

---

1 The full list of skill objectives we formulated for our project is given in Chapter Two.

ability" . . . refers to musical powers or qualifications which may be either innate or acquired. "Ability" takes into account achievement while "aptitude" does not.'

The basis of our test

Standardized music tests were examined as to their appropriateness for pre-trial/post-trial testing of our ESN population (i.e. 119 children spanning the chronological age range of eight to 14 years, with IQs on the WISC scale varying between roughly 50 and 90, and Mental Ages varying between approximately five years and 10 or 11 years). No group-test of musical ability designed specifically for ESN children was available, and no other test was found to be suitable without modification. In view of the evaluation need, it was considered more efficient to modify an existing test than to devise a new one. Bentley's *Measures of Musical Abilities* (1966a) were chosen as a basis for such adaptation because (1) they were devised specifically for younger 'normal' children (aged seven to 14 years), (2) they appeared to be the most effective instrument available for testing young children, and (3) they have been shown to be sensitive to environmental variables including training (Rowntree, 1969). We shall examine these reasons in more detail below.

Prior to Bentley's investigations, no group-test in music had been especially devised for, and standardized upon, young 'normal' children in the age range six to 11. The *Measures* are an attempt to fill this need — i.e. a test battery designed for younger normal children, in this case children aged seven to 14 years (the age range for which norms are given, Bentley, 1966b).

In the existing literature relating to the *Measures*, one finds a general consensus on the tests' evaluative effectiveness. Lehman (1968) states that the Bentley battery is the only adequately standardized aptitude test designed specifically for 'elementary' age children. Shuter (1968) points to the satisfactory reliability of the test as a whole, its promising validity data, and its already extensive popularity. A detailed investigation by Rowntree (1969) led him to conclude that 'the Bentley *Measures of Musical Abilities* are shown as soundly based, valid, reasonably reliable, practicable, and much the most effective test battery available for measuring musical abilities in young children.'

Through his tests, Bentley attempts to measure significant constituent 'musical abilities' from the whole range of potential musical ability, clearly stating (1966b) that his aim is not total comprehensiveness, but the measure of *some* aspects, and in particular those abilities which may be inherited and/or acquired *en passant*, so to speak, and not as the result of training. Indeed, he claims that the abilities disclosed by the *Measures* are in the main innate.

This is a point with which we must take issue, for if Bentley's claim were so, then one would expect the battery to be largely uninfluenced by effects of experience such as specific musical training. In the event, the evidence does not substantiate Bentley's view. To begin with, concerning other musical ability tests it has been shown that test scores can be improved through training (see Holmström, 1963). But more significantly, concerning Bentley's *Measures*, Rowntree (1969) has shown that 'the test scores in Pitch Discrimination and Chord Analysis in particular, and in consequence the Full Battery scores, may be significantly improved by the experience effects of training and practice'. Rowntree's findings, which are based on his investigations using training procedures and recorded practice tests over a period of seven weeks with three principal experimental groups of 10-year-olds and a subsidiary group of seven-year-olds, indeed leave little doubt that the Bentley tests are sensitive to improvement through training, and he concludes that the battery is primarily a measure of 'developed' musical abilities and in fact that it might be used to ascertain the level, or even the rate, of this development.

This being so, the *Measures* are consistent with definitions of 'musical ability' found in the literature. Lehman's definition, for example, has already been singled out, above. Shuter and Taylor (1969) define 'ability' as 'present functioning level'. And Davies (1971) explains: 'Ability involves factors of learning (including practice) and aptitude, which combine to produce a certain level of performance or attainment'. Relating Colwell's definitions in this area to Rowntree's seven-week experience study of the *Measures*, we might even suggest that the *Measures*, can be used as achievement tests. According to Colwell (1970), achievement concerns those aspects which we can assess periodically (weekly, monthly, yearly).[1]

---

1   For a further discussion of definitions, and specifically the difference between aptitude and achievement tests, the reader is referred to Lehman (1968).

The modifications

In this study, in distinct contrast to Bentley's, the population sample comprises ESN children. Thus by declaration we are dealing with the educationally backward. The particular learning problems which are associated with ESN children, and which are discussed elsewhere in this book, obviate any use of the Bentley *Measures* amongst this population without at least some changes in the administration of the tests. We describe the departures which McLeish and Higgs (1967) undertook when testing ESNs (the group in question, i.e. 25 ESN children aged eight to 15, with an average Mental Age of 7.2, were given three music tests including the *Measures*): the testing was done in a special room, with just two children at a time; the tests were presented on tape so that pauses could be introduced for recording answers; time was spent on clarifying instructions; and the tests were given in stages, different parts at different sittings.

Added to this, there are doubts about the *Measures'* suitability for even normal children under eight. Ellingham (1966), Rowntree (1969) and Jack (1967, cited by Rowntree) all note low mean scores among the seven- and eight-year-olds they tested, but in addition they describe a number of administrative problems. Ellingham points to difficulties encountered by seven- and eight-year-olds in recording answers at the given pace, and also implies possible misunderstandings of the concepts involved. Jack, furthermore, is of the opinion that only seven- and eight-year-olds of above-average intelligence can properly comprehend the directions; for other children in this age-group he claims that the instructions would need repeating more than once. And Rowntree found that many of the seven-year-olds he tested failed to understand what was required (despite the fact that test terminology was sometimes explained before the testing) or to cope with the pace of the tests; some even 'broke down'. The consensus of opinion amongst these researchers is that some variation in test procedures is thus necessary with very young children, for instance pre-test instructional sessions, a slower test pace, etc., and Rowntree in fact demonstrates that with additional instruction seven-year-olds can raise their mean scores considerably.

It was thus apparent that the Bentley *Measures* in their present form would not be suitable for use with ESN children, and we therefore undertook to modify the

Measures, in terms of the ESN sample population here investigated. In the main this involved changes in the individual subtests (including length of the battery), changes in the administration of the battery and changes in the method of recording answers.

Before entering into a more detailed discussion of our modifications we shall consider Bentley's own preliminary work as revealed in his Pilot Tests, for aspects of the latter are relevant to the form of our modified battery.

Preliminaries

Bentley's Pilot Tests were concerned with the abilities of memory and pitch discrimination. The pilot pitch discrimination test consisted of thirty pairs of pitch sounds played on the pianoforte, and subjects were to distinguish whether the second of the paired sounds went up, down or remained the same, and were to indicate the direction of movement by writing the appropriate letter — 'U' for 'up', 'D' for 'down' or 'S' for 'same'. The test used only 'musical' intervals such as are normally associated with Western music, i.e. none smaller than the semitone.

In the pilot memory test there were thirty pairs of tunes, again, as in the previous test, played on the pianoforte. The tunes ranged in length from three notes to ten. Subjects were to distinguish whether the paired tunes were the same or different, and to indicate which by writing 'S' or 'D'. Differences concerned pitch only, never note-length, so that rhythm remained constant in each pair.

Bentley found certain limitations in his pilot tests as regards both administration and content. High scores on the pitch test suggested it was too easy and therefore a new pitch discrimination test was prepared in which finer-than-semitone discriminations were required. In the memory test, confusion resulted from the combining of tonal and rhythmic aspects, and it was thus decided that two separate tests should be devised to measure these elements individually. Bentley further resolved: to make all the items in the memory tests the same length (5-note tunes for the tonal memory test, and 4-pulse rhythmic figures for the rhythmic memory test); to introduce a more critical judgement in the memory tests, that of locating exactly where in an item any differences in pitch or rhythm occur; and to make a recording of the battery (including instructions, examples and test items), rather than presenting the tests 'live' as before.

A revised battery thus emerged which initially comprised three tests: Pitch Discrimination, Tonal Memory and Rhythmic Memory. To these Bentley added a fourth, a test of Chord Analysis, reasoning that in the practice of music this judgement, i.e. the perception of concurrent sounds, is also important. The resulting battery comprises, then, four tests in all, proposed by Bentley as measuring some aspects of musical ability.

It now remains to consider in detail how the writer modified the Bentley *Measures*; through these adaptations it was hoped to provide a new battery of musical ability tests suitable for use with ESN children.

Modifications at our pilot stage

In considering how to accommodate our ESN sample, we gave particular attention to: (1) the testing approach with ESNs of McLeish and Higgs (1967 — see again p. 65, above), (2) the difficulties surrounding use of the *Measures* with 'normal' children under eight, (3) the size of our sample, time limitations in the testing schedule, and the nature of our schools' organization, points which favoured group-testing (following the Bentley model) as the testing method, and (4) the youngest and the least intelligent amongst the sample, keeping in mind, particularly, the non-reader.

Following the Bentley model, our 'modified' tests would attempt to assess the same four aspects of musical ability, i.e. pitch discrimination, tonal memory, rhythmic memory and chord analysis.[1] There would, however, be considerable departures in content. The criteria to be considered were: the length of the battery, its use as a group-test, the means of presentation, and the recording of answers.

The nature of our sample dictated that considerable space be given to careful explanations, instructions and examples. This, together with the aspect of limited pupil concentration, and the fact that it was preferable (in the face of time limitations) if the battery could be worked during one sitting, naturally limits the actual item content of our tests. Instead of the 60 items of the Bentley *Measures*, distributed

---

1 While there have been doubts expressed about the use of chord tests with children (see, e.g., Rowntree, 1969), we agreed with Bentley (as also Colwell, 1970), that the judgement involved is important in music-making.

respectively Pitch Discrimination 20 items, Tonal Memory 10, Chord Analysis 20, and Rhythmic Memory 10, our modified battery (in its pilot form) is reduced to 36 items, distributed respectively 12 items, 6, 12 and 6.

Because we wished to retain group-testing, we also probed into the operations necessary to work the test, and the practicalities of recording answers. It was important that the children should understand, by means of the recorded instructions only (we planned to record on tape), what was required, since any further elaboration, as for instance by the test administrator, would interfere with the constancy of the battery. Thus the procedure which we proposed is purposely simple and straightforward, much simpler than that required in the *Measures*, eliminating the need to write numbers or letters, to count, to locate the position of a change or determine the number of notes in a chord. Every item merely requires a choice between two suggested answers, a method which might be seen as consistent with McLeish and Higgs (1967) who note significantly lower scores in their ESN group when the latter faced discriminations more complex than a simple psychophysical choice. We list here the procedure for each of our modified tests:

1. Pitch discrimination — to distinguish whether two consecutively played notes are the same or different.
2. Tonal memory — to distinguish whether two consecutive melodies comprising three notes each are the same or different; the difference involves a change of one note, only, and rhythm is constant throughout the test.
3. Rhythmic memory — to distinguish whether two consecutive rhythms are the same or different; pitch is constant within each item.
4. Chord analysis — to determine whether particular sounds contain only one or more than one note; the number of concurrent notes does not extend beyond a maximum of three.

Since in each of our tests a simple choice is involved, the means of recording answers is also simpler than in the *Measures*. All that is necessary is that the child be able to indicate his choice between the two given answers. Thus, for each item he must mark (by ticking or any other means) one of two adjacent coloured boxes — red, for each pair of notes, melodies or rhythms in the tests which are the 'same', or in the case of chord analysis, when only one note is sounded; yellow, for each pair of notes, melodies or rhythms which are 'different', or again in chord analysis, when more than one note is sounded. The colour order of the boxes is varied throughout each test to discourage any tendency to associate colour with position, or uniformity of order with uniformity in recording answers (see Appendix D).

To simplify the procedure still further, a separate page is available for every answer (again, see Appendix D). Thus, instead of Bentley's single answer form, four separate answer books are used, one for each subtest. To add to the interest, we made the books in different colours — Pitch discrimination, blue; Tonal memory, pink; Chord analysis, green; Rhythmic memory, yellow. All answer pages are numbered, but only as a check for the test administrator to ensure that each child is keeping pace and not turning two pages at once; no reference to the numbers is made during testing, but instead an indication is given (via the recording) when to turn each page.

To maintain constancy for all subjects, the whole pilot battery, including instructions and examples, was recorded on tape. All items were played on the pianoforte. Instructions were repeated frequently, both before and after every item, in order to prompt the memory as to procedure, and practice examples preceded each test.

We now present a more detailed description of our modified battery in its pilot form. Our discussion here will be fairly thorough, since apart from some minor revisions, the pilot battery is essentially the same as our final battery. The notation of the pilot items can be seen in Appendix D. The revisions are described later in this chapter.

Description of our modified battery — pilot form

a. *Pitch discrimination.* Our pilot pitch discrimination test consists of twelve pairs of notes, played on the pianoforte, each note sustained for approximately two seconds. The second note of each pair is separated from the first by two seconds of silence. Test procedure involves identifying (by marking the appropriate coloured box) whether the two notes of a pair are the 'same' (red) or 'different' (yellow); two practice examples, one of a 'same' item and one of a 'different' item, precede the test, and instructions are given both before and after every test item.

The sustaining time for each note is one second longer than in the pitch test of the Bentley *Measures*; also the pause between paired notes is a departure from Bentley's procedure of following one sound immediately by the other. These changes were made in order to slow down the actual presentation of the aural stimuli, and in so doing to try to accommodate the slower responses of the children involved.[1]

The major departure from Bentley's *Measures* involves the actual content of the test. Our pilot pitch test uses, like Bentley's pilot test (and, it must be emphasized, unlike Bentley's final version of his test) only 'musical' intervals. In addition to four unison or 'same' items, we include eight pitch differences from the semitone to the major sixth. Of the eight 'different' items, four involve an upward pitch movement between the two notes of a pair, and four a downward movement. The decision to ignore Bentley's revised test with its finer-than-semitone discrimination (the sounds are created on a sine-wave oscillator), and rather, to concentrate on the greater-than-semitone judgements necessary to discriminate 'Western' intervals, will be seen as a fundamental difference between the pitch test of the Bentley *Measures* and the modified version being discussed. This difference, contingent on our assumption on the nature of an ESN sample, relates to two considerations, firstly that the test should not be too difficult, and secondly that the test should avoid, as much as possible, any element of strangeness. It was also felt that, although critical pitch judgements might be important to good intonation, this is not really a relevant enough justification (in terms of our music programme) for including finer-than-semitone discriminations with our ESN sample. We need not, then, go into the possible problems and criticisms surrounding the use of smaller-than-semitone differences.

Thus, the material chosen for our modified pitch test is similar to that which was found to be relatively easy for Bentley's pilot sample of young 'normal' children. Also, it is material which is familiar, in as much as it comprises ingredients from Western music. Furthermore, it is played on a familiar instrument, the pianoforte.

This aspect of familiarity is considered to be an important one, for it means that our modified test, in using only

---

[1] The successful imaging by children of sounds through three seconds of silence has been demonstrated by Hickman (1968).

'musical' intervals, involves cultural learning. As Holmström (1963) points out, a test is more subject to experience effects the more 'musical' elements it comprises. Thus, our test might be seen as a relevant instrument in evaluating the effects of training (or cultural conditioning) through music programmes.

We should also mention the compass of our test, which is much more restricted than in the comparable Bentley test. In Bentley's pilot test the range extends from A below middle C to E two octaves and a third above middle C, whereas in our modified test, the range extends from D a tone above middle C to C an octave above middle C. The smaller compass in the latter test restricts the pitch sounds heard to those within the general vocal range of young children.

It is commonly accepted that pitch discrimination is easier within the vocal compass than outside it, and taking into account such matters as the possible assistance of sub-vocalization in pitch judgements, and the accommodation of 'growlers' within a somewhat lower range than the recognized 'treble' of children's songs, we might suggest that the range chosen for our modified test is large enough both to accommodate diverse vocal compasses and to allow for 'musical' variety amongst the intervals. All the intervals are different and without a common note, aspects which, considering our sample's restricted attention span, are thought to be preferable to any constancy which might be gained from the use of a reference tone.

b. *Tonal memory*. Our pilot tonal memory test consists of six items, played on the pianoforte, each item consisting of two 3-note tunes separated by three crotchet rests. Rhythm is constant throughout the test, all the notes being of equal length (crotchets), played at approximately M.M. $\downarrow$ = 52.

Test procedure involves identifying (by marking the appropriate coloured box) whether the two tunes of an item are the 'same' (red) or 'different' (yellow); two practice examples, one of a 'same' item and one of a 'different' item, precede the test, and instructions are given both before and after every item.

Our modified tonal test is similar in content to the corresponding test of the Bentley *Measures* (final form). Major departures involve certain simplifications and an overall slowing-down in presentation:

1. Three-note tunes are used instead of the 5-note tunes of Bentley's test.

2. There are six items (instead of Bentley's ten), three comprising paired tunes which are the 'same', and three, tunes which are 'different', and the procedure involves distinguishing which are which; changes in the 'different' items occur on the third, second and first notes respectively. In contrast, the Bentley items comprise paired tunes which are all 'different', and the procedure involves identifying the exact position of a changed note in each pair, the changes being equally distributed amongst the five notes of the tunes.

3. In the modified test, all the changes involve the interval of a third, whereas in the Bentley test the changes involve the smaller differences of a semitone or a wholetone. The larger interval is chosen in the modified test in order that the change in a 'different' item might be made more obvious.

4. The speed of playing in the modified test is about half that of the Bentley test, and the two tunes of an item are separated from each other by three crotchet rests.

5. The modified test is played on a pianoforte, whereas the Bentley test is played on a pipe organ (using 8' and 4' flute stops). In both the modified and the Bentley test the range extends from D above middle C to A above middle C.

c. *Chord analysis*. Our pilot chord analysis test consists of twelve items, played on the pianoforte, each item comprising either a single note, or a two- or three-note chord which is sustained for three seconds.

Test procedure involves identifying (by marking the appropriate coloured box) whether just one note is sounded (red) or two or three notes together (yellow); three practice examples, one of a single note, one of a two-note chord and one of a three-note chord, precede the test, and instructions are given both before and after every item.

The modified chord analysis test is similar in content to the corresponding test of the Bentley *Measures* (final form), but again as with our tonal memory test, there are simplifications:

1. The modified test comprises both single notes and two- and three-note chords, the number of concurrent notes never extending beyond a maximum of three, whereas Bentley's test consists of two-, three-, and also four-note chords, but does not include any single notes.

2. There are twelve items in the modified test (instead of

Bentley's 20), four single notes, five 2-note chords and three 3-note chords, and the procedure involves distinguishing the chords from the single notes. In contrast, the Bentley items are all chords and the procedure involves identifying the number of notes in each, i.e. two, three or four.[1]

3. There are fewer pungent dissonances in the modified test as compared to the Bentley test, owing to the exclusion of major 7ths and minor 2nds. We might cite, here, Rowntree (1969), who notes that strong facial and vocal reactions were common 'against' the dissonant chords of Bentley's items 2, 9, 11 and 13, particularly in the remedial classes or low streams. Thus, in our modified test the possibility was considered that pungent dissonances might very well distract and even confuse our ESN sample; indeed, because these children are ESN, and because they live at a time of mass communication when the most predictable musical diet comprises fairly simple harmonies and generally consonant sounds (i.e. 'popular' music), they are perhaps unlikely to be conditioned to more selective aural stimuli such as pungent dissonances.

4. The modified test is played on a pianoforte, whereas the Bentley test is played on a pipe organ (using an 8' open diapason stop).

In the modified test, as in the Bentley test, no two adjacent items have any one note in common; this is to avoid any possible feeling of tonality which might affect discrimination.

d. *Rhythmic memory*. Our pilot rhythmic memory test consists of six items, played on the pianoforte, each item consisting of two 2-pulse rhythmic patterns separated by two crotchet rests. The speed of playing is approximately M.M. ♩ = 40.

Test procedure involves identifying (by marking the appropriate coloured box) whether the two rhythms of an item are the 'same' (red) or 'different' (yellow); two practice examples, one of a 'same' item and one of a 'different' item, precede the test, and instructions are given both before and after every item.

Our modified rhythmic memory test is similar in content

---

1 The simplification of method in our modified chord test might be seen as consistent with evidence that a child's judgement of the number of notes in a chord is a function of the tonal composition of the chord itself (Hickman, 1968).

to the corresponding test of the Bentley *Measures* (final form). As in our modified tonal memory test, major departures involve certain simplifications and an overall slowing-down in presentation:

1. Two-pulse rhythmic patterns are used instead of the 4-pulse patterns of Bentley's test; in addition, the tempo is not counted out vocally before each item is played.

2. There are six items (instead of Bentley's ten), two comprising paired rhythms which are the 'same', and four rhythms which are 'different', and the procedure involves distinguishing which are which; changes in the 'different' items are equally distributed between the two pulses. In the Bentley test, on the other hand, there are two items with paired rhythms the 'same', and eight which are 'different', and the procedure involves distinguishing which are which, then identifying the exact position of the rhythmic alteration in each 'different' pair; the changes are equally distributed amongst the four pulses of the rhythms.

3. The speed of playing in the modified test is about half that of the Bentley test.

4. The modified test is played on a pianoforte whereas the Bentley test is played on a pipe organ (using 8' small diapason and 2' fifteenth stops).

In both the modified and the Bentley test there is no change of pitch within an item, but in the interests of variety, the pitch level is changed between items. In both tests, also, the two rhythms of an item are separated from each other by two crotchet rests.

Recording and reproduction

In contrast to the Bentley *Measures* (as marketed), each of our modified tests uses a pianoforte to create the sounds. The most obvious advantage in the instrument's use and the primary reason for choosing it here are its familiarity to the majority of children, and the fact that such familiarity is perhaps of particular importance in terms of our ESN sample. That the pianoforte was, in fact, familiar to the children under study was more than borne out during testing. On repeated testing occasions, usually during the examples of the first test, children voiced their recognition of the instrument — and with obvious satisfaction — asking such questions as: 'That's a piano, Miss, isn't it?' 'Is that you playing the piano, Miss?' Many also eagerly pointed out their desire to learn the instrument.

A second consideration, perhaps of almost equal importance for our sample, is aural interest, for an instrument such as the pianoforte whose tonal structure changes according to pitch and loudness is of more interest to the ear than an instrument devoid of harmonics such as, for example, the pure tone sine-wave oscillator which is not affected by changes in timbre. It might be suggested that it is of advantage to avoid boredom particularly where concentration might be weaker.

The main disadvantages in the piano's use for tests are technical and reflect the specific quality of this instrument, i.e. its sensitivity to touch or velocity of key depression which enables different volume levels to be produced through the physical contact between fingers and keys. Thus Bentley's contention concerns the piano's use in the chord test — the problem of ensuring equality of volume amongst chord notes, concern at the rapid fading of a piano note soon after it has been struck. Because of such drawbacks, Bentley resorted to the use of a pipe organ instead of a pianoforte in his chord test.

Looking at Bentley's first criticism in more detail, one can defend on two grounds the use of a pianoforte in our modified tests. Firstly, even if test reproduction approaches perfection originally, this does not preclude that acoustic problems might arise when the test is actually administered (sympathetic resonance, especially during the Bentley Chord test, was a common problem met by Rowntree, 1969). Secondly, the nature of our modified chord test is such that an 'aural impression' is probably adequate to distinguish single notes from the two- or three-note combinations of the chords. Indeed, both content and procedure in our chord test seem to demand less precision inthe creation of the sounds than is required in the comparable Bentley test where all the items are chords, consisting of 2, 3 and also 4 notes in combination, and where the procedure involves identifying the actual number of notes in each (this is without even considering how tonal composition might affect the estimate of notes).

Bentley's concern with the rapid drop in intensity of a piano note soon after it is struck, i.e. even within three seconds, can also be minimized if impressions are again considered relevant. It has been pointed out by Briggs (1951) that when the intensity of a piano note decreases, the aural impression is not proportional to the actual decrease, but is rather about one-fifth of this. Briggs also considers that because there is not 'the build-up of power' connected with sustaining instruments, sufficient room reverberation can improve the piano's tone. And we refer to Sergeant (1969) who from his studies of pitch perception (specifically absolute pitch) concludes that transients form a more important cue than do partials.

It perhaps goes without saying that our modified pitch test, in using 'musical' intervals, can be produced quite adequately using a traditional musical instrument such as a pianoforte, in contrast to the Bentley pitch test (final version) which requires a sine-wave oscillator.

The procedure for our modified tests is, as we have seen, simpler than that required in the Bentley *Measures*, and, like our modified chord test, in particular, seemed overall to demand less precision in the creation of the sounds. Even so, every effort was made to be precise, pianistically, in producing the music of our tests. Except for the differences involved in the 'different' items, the paired notes, tunes and rhythms were played as similarly as possible, i.e. in respect of tempo, duration of the notes and volume. The undue prominence of any note was avoided as carefully as the pianist's skill and the instrument's mechanics permitted; in terms of the instrument, this meant avoiding notes (particularly in the chord test) which were noticeably resonant in comparison to others, a consideration which had some bearing, then, on the actual musical content of the tests.

We have noted that, to maintain constancy in administration, our modified test battery was recorded on tape. The recordings were made entirely by the present writer, for which reason the pianoforte held a further attraction, the writer being a pianist. The instrument used for the tests was an upright, built around 1912 by a well-known German maker, and kept in good condition; it is over-strung, with under-damper action and iron frame.

The tapings were made in a private house in a rectangular brick-walled room, measuring about 20 feet long by 12 feet wide by 8 feet high (shape and size meet Briggs's standards for good tone production, 1951, 1967). The recording room was carpeted, but not wall-to-wall, and the piano stood on the exposed wooden floor at the perimeter, about six inches away from the wall.

A four-track, three-speed tape recorder of reputable make

was used to record our tests. As judged subjectively, we gained the best results on tape by (1) placing the microphone on a cushion, set on a low table about the height of the piano bench and at a distance of approximately three feet behind the pianist, and (2) playing the sounds with the piano lid down and the soft pedal depressed (which appeared to reduce the number of audible harmonics). It was also found that the instructions could be recorded using the same volume level setting on the recorder, and sitting at the same distance from the microphone, as used to perform the music; thus the procedure, whenever speech was required, was for the writer to turn sideways on the piano bench and to project her voice towards the microphone. The tests were recorded at a speed of 3¾ inches per second.

Administrative procedure

Our modified tests were administered by the writer using the same tape recorder for playback as was used in the actual recording. The procedure adopted in the testing followed as nearly similar a pattern in the individual schools as conditions permitted. Thus a few words of introduction from the writer informed the children that they were going to listen to some musical sounds and write some answers in some books, and that the tape recorder would tell them exactly what to do. They were also told that they should write down only what *they* thought the answers should be, and should not worry about their neighbour's answers. The tape was then turned on and the modified test battery was worked through in one session, with breaks of three or four minutes between tests to allow for the distribution and collection of answer books. The same order of presentation was used as for the Bentley *Measures*, i.e. pitch discrimination, tonal memory, chord analysis and rhythmic memory.

To enable our modified tests to be worked by these children as described — that is, solely in response to the tape recording and without interference by the administrator — certain revisions to the content of our pilot tests (particularly to the instructions) were required; these will be explained later when the results of the pilot testing are discussed. It suffices to say that misunderstandings arose during the actual working of our pilot tests, necessitating verbal explanations from the administrator over and above those given on the tape, and this in turn interfered with the tests' constancy. Effort was made to rectify these problems in the subsequent revisions.

The conditions for testing varied according to the school. On most occasions it was possible to test the children in their own classrooms, but sometimes school halls or special subject rooms, such as those for woodwork or domestic science, had to be used. As might be expected power-points were located in various places, not always at the front of the room, and thus it was not always possible for children to sit facing the loudspeaker. In fact children often faced in a variety of directions since non-formal grouping was usual in all the schools participating, and furthermore we tried to separate the children as much as possible to avoid co-operative work on the tests. In the event, close observation of the classes revealed that aurally it appeared to make no difference where the children sat relative to the loudspeaker.

Class teachers helped in the supervision during testing.

Results of our pilot testing

The pilot tests of our modified battery were administered at a special school for ESN girls (which we called Brockton School) in Metropolitan Merseyside. The initial testing involved six subjects, two from each of the chronological age groups 8/9, 10/11 and 12/13, each pair including a high and a low IQ. The range of IQs on the Stanford-Binet scale [1] was from 51 to 78.

The tests, complete with instructions, were presented on tape, and answer books were provided for each girl, a separate book for each test.

The whole battery took approximately one hour to administer, which included a 10-minute break after the second test, and time devoted to preliminaries such as distribution and collection of answer books, pencils and rubbers. On the whole the children attended fairly well considering they took the tests at one sitting, but they did tire as the battery progressed. Only one, the youngest of the group and a low IQ, showed obvious signs of restlessness.

Results of our initial pilot testing

There were only two considered failures (i.e. with less than 50 per cent correct) in the whole battery of 36 items and these were the two lowest IQs: Pitch test scores ranged from four correct answers to the maximum possible 12, with mean

---

1   See Terman and Merrill (1961).

score of 8.5; Tonal memory scores ranged from one correct answer to three (half the possible maximum), with mean score of 2.5; Chord analysis scores ranged from four correct answers to 11 (12 being the maximum possible), with mean score of 6.5; Rhythmic memory scores ranged from two correct answers to four (six being the maximum possible), with mean score of 3.2.

a. *Revision of our pilot tests*. The generally high scores of our pitch test suggested that it was too easy; intervals (i.e. 'different' notes) from the semitone to the major sixth had been included, and the revision consisted in eliminating the larger intervals (fourths, fifths and sixths) so that the largest interval included would now be a major third, while the smallest would still remain the semitone.

Our chord analysis test, perhaps the most difficult of the tests to understand, was thought to be rather too long because of the detailed introductory explanations which were required in addition to the twelve test items. The revision consisted in omitting two items (2 and 9) and altering one 3-note chord (item 5) to include a wider interval spread; the latter alteration was made because of the initial similarity of the chord with item 10 (see Appendix D).

Our other tests, tonal and rhythmic memory, remained unchanged.

b. *Revision of the instructions*. We found during the initial testing that we had erred on the side of completeness; the taped directions were too repetitious and lengthy for the number of test items in the battery. Indeed, most subjects became bored with the verbal passages soon after the first subtest, and often ignored the repeated instructions after each item. Our revision consisted in eliminating the directions after the third and subsequent items in each subtest, and the often repeated phrase 'Let's go on'.

Results of our second pilot testing

The same six subjects were tested with our revised battery approximately one week after the initial testing. As before, the tests complete with instructions were presented on tape, and answer books provided for each girl.

The administration of the battery again took approximately one hour. The children were responsive and quiet to begin with, but showed obvious signs of boredom at being retested.

There were three considered failures (i.e. with less than 50 per cent correct) in the whole battery of 34 items, two of the failures being the two lowest IQs: Pitch test scores ranged from five correct answers to 11 (12 being the maximum possible), with mean score of 7.7; Tonal memory scores ranged from two correct answers to three (half the possible maximum), with mean score of 2.8; Chord analysis scores ranged from two correct answers to seven (10 being the maximum possible), with mean score of 4.8; Rhythmic memory scores ranged from one correct answer to four (6 being the maximum possible), with mean score of two.

a. *Further revision of our pilot tests*. In our tonal and rhythmic memory tests many of the children were not able to comprehend an item as being made up of two separate tunes or patterns, the second tune being played after a period of silence; indeed, some seemed to think that both parts of an item were contained in the first tune or pattern and tried to answer before the second tune was heard. In order to clarify which was the first tune or pattern, and which was the second, verbal prompting was necessary during the administration of the battery. It was thus decided to incorporate this prompting in the tape recording, with the result that the rests (indicating the silences) are eliminated from the final version of the notated tests.

b. *Further revision of the instructions*. We still felt that the instructions overall were too wordy and repetitious for the majority of ESN children; indeed, continual reiteration of the directions appeared to be unnecessary, for once the children had grasped the procedure for each test they tended either to ignore subsequent repetitions of the instructions, or else to mouth them along with the speaker on the tape.

Our revision consisted of an overall trimming of the directions. For clarity, an instruction was added which informed the children when to tick each answer. It was also thought advisable to pause (1) after this new direction, and (2) after the instruction to turn the page; waits of 10 seconds and seven seconds respectively were thus incorporated. Such procedures should free one from using the temporary stop on the tape recorder.

c. *Final version of our tests*. When the revisions to the pilot tests were complete, our modified battery in its final form was recorded on tape. A cassette recording of the complete Modified Test Battery can be obtained from the NFER Publishing Company. Details of the notation of our tests, together with the text of instructions, will be found in Appendix D of this book.

Reliability

Since our Modified Battery differs essentially from the Bentley *Measures*, being in fact a new test, it is necessary to examine its basic psychometric quality. To obtain a measure of test-retest reliability for the final version of our Modified Battery, we tested another sample of girls from the pilot school, Brockton School, in this case 15 children drawn in equal numbers from each of the chronological age groups 8/9, 10/11 and 12/13, with an in-group IQ range of approximately 58 to 75 on the Stanford-Binet scale; the test and retest were administered approximately two weeks apart to minimize any possible memory effects.

A further measure of reliability, internal consistency, was obtained by applying a variant of the split-half method, the Kuder-Richardson Formula 20 (Richardson and Kuder, 1939) to the initial test scores and the retest scores of our project's 59 experimental and 60 contrast children, separately; in this case the test and retest were administered approximately one year apart.

Table 2 summarizes the reliability data on our Modified Battery by presenting the two types of reliability coefficient discussed above.

The reliability coefficients for the total scores on the Modified Battery range from ·67 to ·81 (median coefficient = ·75). The individual subtests show varying degrees of reliability, but the range of median coefficients is quite small (subtest 1, median coefficient = ·51; subtest 2, median coefficient = ·48; subtest 3, median coefficient = ·56; subtest 4, median coefficient = ·50).

Bentley (1963) points out that the shortness of his battery (comprising a total of 60 items) necessarily affects reliability. It may be expected, therefore, that our Modified Battery, by including only 34 items, will have a lower reliability than the Bentley. In this connection, it might be useful to examine the reliability figures obtained for the Bentley tests.

Table 2: Reliability coefficients (test-retest and internal) based on our pilot school group of 15 and our Dunbar and Hudson samples

	TEST 1	TEST 2	TEST 3	TEST 4	TEST Total
Test-Retest Pilot School	·48	·59	·84	·52	·67
K-R$_{20}$, Dunbar Test	·44	·48	·56	·55	·74
K-R$_{20}$, Hudson Test	·51	·29	·44	·50	·75
K-R$_{20}$, Dunbar Retest	·73	·52	·61	·29	·81
K-R$_{20}$, Hudson Retest	·69	·41	·54	·40	·75

Test-retest reliability studies of the Bentley 'Measures'

Table 3 summarizes reliability data from four studies of the Bentley *Measures*, that by Bentley himself (1963), and also Rowntree (1969), Jack (cited by Rowntree) and McLeish (1968). Data from our own study appear for comparison in the fifth column. Note that neither Jack nor Rowntree present reliability data for the separate sub-tests, but have calculated a *range* of coefficients for the Full Battery based on different age-groups, and, in the case of Jack, combined age and sex groups. McLeish presents only a Full Battery score which is based on combined age and intelligence groups.

The test-retest coefficients obtained with our Modified Battery reach the five per cent level of significance in the case of Tonal Memory and Rhythmic Memory, and the one per cent level in the case of Chord Analysis and the Full Battery score (with degrees of freedom = 13, $r \geqslant ·51$, $p < ·05$; $r \geqslant ·64$, $p < ·01$). Only in the case of Pitch Discrimination does the reliability coefficient fall below the 5 per cent level. Clearly, then, this is the sub-test where results will be most suspect.

It is difficult to make direct comparisons between reliability as estimated for our Modified Battery, and the other figures set out in Table 3. The age-range of our children, eight to 13 years, is rather wider than in the reference studies (excepting McLeish); our test-retest interval is shorter than

Table 3: Test-retest reliability coefficients obtained from other studies of the Bentley 'Measures' and the Dickinson modification

	Bentley[1]	Jack[2]	Rowntree[3]	McLeish[4]	Dickinson Modified Battery[5]
Pitch Discrimination	·75	—	—	—	·48
Tonal Memory	·53	—	—	—	·59
Chord Analysis	·71	—	—	—	·84
Rhythmic Memory	·57	—	—	—	·52
Full Battery	·84	·47—·85	·49—·63	·83	·67

1 Bentley — based on N = 90; age-range 9 yrs. 10 mos. — 11 yrs. 9 mos.; 4-month interval between test and retest.
2 Jack — N = 600+; age-range 7—10 yrs.; test-retest interval, within 1 month.
3 Rowntree — N = 443; age-range 7+ to 10+; 4- to 5-month interval between test and retest.
4 McLeish — N = 105 (25 ESN children aged 8—15 yrs.; 50 primary school children aged 9—10 yrs.; 30 secondary modern school children aged 12—13 yrs.); one-year interval between test and retest. We note that variations in procedure were necessary to test the ESN children (see above, p.65).
5 See Table 2.

Bentley's and Rowntree's; but most noteworthy is the depressed IQ level of our sample. Only the present study estimates reliability specifically for a homogeneously sub-normal group, inevitably involving the diminished attention span, lowered persistence levels, and questionable 'set' towards the test, which one would expect to characterize such a group. Taking into account these considerations, one may however suggest that in relation to the type of subject tested, the number of test items included (34) and the particular function of our test (i.e. a measure of musical achievement for curriculum evaluation), the figures for our Modified Battery indicate a generally acceptable degree of reliability.

Validity

It is assumed that, despite the modifications, there is sufficient overlap of our Modified Battery and Bentley's *Measures* to make similar generalizations as to validity. For reference, however, it is perhaps useful to cite a few examples in which test scores for our Modified Battery relate to *observations* of a pupil's musical ability or achievement during our programme's operation at Dunbar.

a. One boy in particular comes to mind, child IIIB7, IQ 78 (WISC), age 147 months at the start of the programme.[1] In all the activities he appeared to show ability. He gained 30 out of 34 marks on initial testing, and a perfect score on post-programme testing with the Modified Battery (the only child in either the contrast or experimental samples to gain a perfect score). His manual dexterity was good and led to his proficiency (i.e. achievement of physical set, guided response and mechanism — see Chapter Six) on a total of eight instruments. His ability to perform instrumental music (i.e. in rote performances, rehearsed reading, sightreading and improvising — see again Chapter Six) was judged to be outstanding. His sense of rhythm and grasp of notation was well developed, to the extent, in fact, that he was often asked by his teacher to demonstrate for the class during sight-

---

1   To ensure anonymity of the children we used an identity code, which worked as follows: a Roman numeral identifies the group to which the child belonged (either I, II or III, youngest to oldest age-groups); a letter identifies the sex of the child; and an Arabic numeral identifies the particular child in the group.

reading exercises.

b. A girl in the youngest group provides a further example, child IG6, IQ 80 (WISC), age 109 months at the start of the programme. She gained 25 marks on the initial testing and 31 marks on the post-testing with the Modified Battery. She achieved physical set, guided response and mechanism on a total of seven instruments. Furthermore, her ability to perform instrumental music (in the areas noted in the above example) was judged to be excellent, and indeed she was often called upon by her teacher to demonstrate this performance proficiency in front of the class. She also learned songs easily, and sang them on pitch.

c. Child IIBIO, IQ 83 (WISC), age 144 months at the start of the programme, likewise appeared to show ability in the musical activities. He gained 27 marks on the initial testing and 29 marks on the post-testing with the Battery. He achieved physical set, guided response and mechanism on a total of seven instruments, and demonstrated high standards of proficiency in his performance of instrumental music, particularly in the parts he performed in two extended works learned by his class.

d. Child IIIB2, IQ 68 (WISC), age 147 months at the start of the programme, gained 28 marks on the initial testing, and 33 marks on the post-testing with the Battery. He achieved physical set, guided response and mechanism on a total of six instruments, and demonstrated high standards of proficiency in his performance of instrumental music, particularly during Christmas and Easter concerts. He also learned songs easily and sang them on pitch.

e. Just as the above examples of high achievement appear to relate to high musical ability test scores, so, too, observations of poor ability appear to relate to low scores on our tests. For example, child IBI, IQ 71 (WISC), age 127 months at the start of the programme, gained only 1 mark on the initial testing and 1 mark on the post-testing with the Battery. His manual dexterity was poor, and he managed to achieve physical set and guided response on only three instruments, and mechanism on none. At the same time his ability to perform instrumental music was judged to be only fair, and indeed his performances were accomplished only after much guidance from his teacher.

f. Similarly, child IIGI, IQ 58 (WISC), age 126 months at the start of the programme, appeared to be a poor achiever. She gained 18 marks on the initial testing and 16 marks on the post-testing with the Battery. Of the three instruments she attempted, she achieved physical set and guided response on only two, and mechanism on only one. Furthermore, her ability to perform instrumental music was judged to be of a low standard.

The list could be extended by further examples but we have chosen the most relevant and representative.

Suitability

The appropriateness of our Modified Battery for the sample population is perhaps revealed by the response of our pupils to working the tests. On the whole the children appeared to derive pleasure from the task, and in fact were often keen to tell the tester how easy it seemed to them. As possible reasons for this response, we might propose that the threat of failure was not readily apparent to the children because they were able to understand the instructions and because they found the actual answering task well within their capabilities.

In the present chapter we have described the development and design of the musical ability test used in our investigation. Whilst we have included a reliability study, we have not yet discussed the testing results proper, i.e. the comparison of scores between our experimental and contrast children. These will be examined, together with other evaluation results, in the next chapter.

Chapter Six

The Evaluation

The aims and objectives of this study, and our evaluation procedure, were discussed in Chapter Two. It now remains to discuss our evaluation instruments and the data we obtained with them.

As we noted earlier, data were collected from four areas associated with our *illuminative* approach to evaluation: observation, questionnaires, documentary sources and tests. Since only our tryout population experienced the programme, we reaffirm that our evidence is *primarily* internal, lacking objective comparison with an external group — though, as we know, in one area, the domain of musical ability testing, a comparison group was involved. Thus the quality of our evidence varies along the spectrum from that which is more prone to subjective error to that which is less prone.

We readily admit to limitations in our assessment, because our evaluation approach relies to such a large extent on personal interpretation; and the observer role, in particular, while a device for securing information, cannot be completely severed from the observer's self. But obviously, we made every effort to eliminate invalidating influences, and to this end we used certain 'precautionary tactics' as advocated by Parlett and Hamilton (1972): different techniques were employed to cross-check findings; outside consultants were petitioned to check the interpretations; documentation was thorough, including details of our research techniques, our theoretical framework and our rationale; and certain evidence was presented to allow a corresponding assessment by the reader. We also searched the data collection situation for potentially contaminating factors such as: reactive effects to the observer's presence; selective perception by the observer;

ethnocentrism; any tendency by the observer to 'over-rapport' with the subjects; investigator self-consciousness, anxiety, bias; and possible distorting influences on reports by the subjects (i.e. questionable informant reliability, his mental set, idiosyncratic factors such as momentary moods and circumstances, ulterior motives) – see further in McCall and Simmons (1969). A final check was made by constantly comparing the data as derived from our different collecting techniques and different participants (here, the constant comparative method of qualitative analysis (Glaser, 1969) served as a model).

At the other end of our data spectrum, the test data, we were also cautious. In testing propositions (whether they were pre-specified, discovered while in the field, or post-programme propositions), we tried to satisfy the following criteria: to define precisely what was being measured and how; to define the relevant population samples; to search the data for similarly contaminating influences; and finally, to analyse the distribution of our evidence. In the actual data collection, we tried to sample each participant or each event within a certain time period, as relevant to the proposition.

From the total data we gathered using illuminative evaluation techniques, categories of analysis were defined, and progressively focused in relation to our growing body of information. This delimiting of categories (Glaser, 1969) isolated three which provide points of departure for our evaluative discussions: (1) the teachers' ability to cope with the music teaching, (2) pupil response, and (3) pupil musical achievements. These, of course, are directly related to our programme: whilst categories (2) and (3) may be modified by (1), all three are modified by the programme itself, and are thus a reflection of programme suitability.

Ultimately, though, our evaluation approach looks to general principles, and in our final chapter we shall postulate some hypotheses about music teaching by the musically non-specialist teacher of ESNs, generally.

Catalogue of our evaluation instruments

Since our investigation is two-dimensional with both teacher and pupil emphases, we have several sorts of data to consider respective to each. Briefly, the data on our teachers are based on observation and questionnaires, and thus constitute what might be termed 'soft' data. Our pupil data, on the other hand, comprise both 'soft' and 'hard' data, being based on observation, questionnaires and documentary sources, and at the other end of the spectrum, tests. The specifics of these evaluation instruments are discussed below.

Observation

A continuous record of the day-to-day events of our music sessions was kept through *in situ* observation. The writer attended every lesson as an observer and codified what she saw and heard, using, in the field situation, specially devised observation sheets (244 in all), which when completed served both as lesson summaries and as aids to recollection for the later detailed lesson write-ups. The observation sheets were divided into several sections, concerning: (1) class reactions, (2) teacher difficulties, (3) pupil instrumental achievement, (4) behaviour problems, (5) extent of topic coverage, and (6) a 'capsule' appraisal (see the format in Appendix E). Brief memos about each lesson were made on the back of each sheet.

While only overt, surface behaviours were recorded through such observations, nevertheless they did help to identify some of the teaching problems which we encountered in the present project, and on the basis of which revisions were made in our programme. From the 244 lesson summaries and write-ups, we coded incidents into our three categories of analysis.

The observational data on teacher response were examined in terms of four criteria determined from the data: attitude towards the music teaching, confidence, understanding of the lesson material and proficiency in the music teaching.

The observational data on pupil response were examined in terms of four levels selected from Bloom, Krathwohl and Masia's taxonomy of affective objectives (1964): willingness to receive, acquiescence in responding, willingness to respond and satisfaction in response.

The observational data on pupil achievement ('observational' because although we were testing propositions, the data here stemmed from observations) were examined in terms of four of our pre-specified skill objectives (see again Chapter Two): the ability to play a musical instrument, the ability to help make a musical instrument, the ability to identify three treble staff pitches, and the ability to perform instrumental music. The first ability, as we have noted, was assessed in terms of three of Simpson's psychomotor objectives, namely, physical set, guided response and mechanism.

The third ability was assessed using two pitch notation 'quizzes'. And the fourth ability was assessed in terms of four instrumental activities, i.e. rote performance, music reading based on rehearsal, sightreading and improvisation.

More will be said concerning these observational tools when we discuss our results.

Questionnaires

Again, data were collected at both teacher and pupil levels. Two questionnaires were devised for our teachers, Questionnaire I, which we gave them at three intervals during the programme, and Questionnaire II, which we submitted at the end of our experiment. Both questionnaires (see Appendix F) were a combination of fixed and free response formats, with the emphasis on the latter. Their purpose was to determine such aspects as the teachers' attitude to the teaching; any anxieties they may have had; what they thought about the programme; what value, if any, they accorded it; how they viewed their pupils' responses; and what unexpected comments (compared to the writer's observations) they might make. Questionnaire II also included a checklist which summarized possible non-musical effects of the programme, and which the teachers were asked to complete in respect of each pupil. (A checkmark was to indicate an improvement. The aspects listed were: motor control; pronunciation or speech; auditory, visual, and tactile perceptiveness; mental alertness; memory; attention span and concentration; co-operation and social integration; self-confidence; acceptance of responsibility, independence.) Questionnaires were thought to be the most appropriate means of obtaining our information because the teachers, being hard-pressed for time and under a certain strain just by participating, were thus enabled to complete this information at their leisure.

Besides the formal questionnaires we submitted to our teachers, we also devised a set of questions for our pupils (see Appendix G). This was given before the end of the project and was intended as written work about the music, the teachers asking the questions verbally in class and the children writing down their replies. The material here contributes to our category on pupil response.

Documentary sources

In addition to the questionnaire replies, practical examples of the children's work included their drawings about the music classes, and a tape of Group 2's performance of *The Three Bears* (i.e. the musical story we discussed earlier, by Nordoff and Robbins). The examples of art work are relevant to the category pupil response, and the tape performance to the category pupil achievement.

Tests

Results from psychometric tests, i.e. our Modified Battery, constitute the 'hard' data end of our spectrum of evidence. These, as we have seen, are tests of musical ability, prepared as a measure of another pre-specified skill objective (see Chapter Two), 'the ability to perceive pitch, melody, rhythm and harmony'. Whilst we have discussed our Battery in some detail in Chapter Five, we might reaffirm two points: that the tests were given to both experimental and contrast pupils on pre-programme and post-programme occasions (with a one-year interval between); and that the type of ability test developed by Bentley (1966a), and on which our Modified Battery is based, is viewed as a descriptive instrument which is sensitive to environmental variables including training.

Assessment and interpretation of teacher response

Although for our purposes of analysis, we consider teacher and pupil responses separately, it is of course axiomatic (as we suggested earlier in this chapter) that 'success' or 'failure' of the programme results from a complex interaction process between programme and teacher, programme and pupil, and teacher and pupil. In many respects the last, two-way flow process between teacher and pupil is most interesting. A given teacher response (to the programme) may communicate itself to the pupil who then responds *to the teacher's 'response'* (which of course functions as a 'stimulus'). Similarly a given pupil response(s) (to the programme) may communicate itself to the teacher who responds to the 'stimulus' elicited by the pupil. Teacher and pupil, then, are often responding to phenomenologically based reactions on the part of the other which creates a complexity in the response chain which may be very difficult to record and analyse. We chose to limit the parameters of both teacher and pupil response, while being fully cognizant of the probable dynamic character of the process.

Observations on the teachers' ability to cope with the music teaching

A full reporting of our evidence would be too protracted here. In the original reports, we supplemented our observations with verbatim extracts from our field diary, but here we shall concentrate on summary views of our data.

In this category we were interested not only in the practical evidence of coping, but also in the concomitant mental set. We must emphasize that while the teachers' *personal* standards of success were operating and thus there might be discrepancies between teacher opinion and that of the investigator, we were not so much interested in the 'reality' of the situation as in what the teachers' responses told us about how they coped, both actively and mentally, with the programme teaching.

The number of lessons eventually taught by each of our teachers was extensive (Teacher 1—58 lessons; Teacher 2—90; Teacher 3—96). It may be recalled that one of the terms of our project required immediate termination of the lessons in the event of any serious signs of failure. A preliminary assessment of teaching effectiveness suggests therefore an overall pattern of success. We carried out a more exhaustive examination in terms of the criteria we mentioned earlier: attitude towards the music teaching, confidence, understanding of the lesson material and proficiency in the music teaching. The indicators we used to appraise the last property include: clarity in the teaching, skill in rehearsal techniques, accurate and demonstrative cueing, conscientious use of controlling techniques such as counting, etc.

We shall now discuss briefly the performance pattern of each of our teachers.

a. *Teacher 1.* Out of 58 lessons given to Group 1, 56 were taught by Teacher 1, and the remaining two lessons by the Headmaster when the class teacher was absent at the start of the project.

Our observations, supported by comments from the questionnaires, infer that this teacher was not altogether happy in meeting the commitments of our programme:

'Maybe better if *you* took the lessons.' (Questionnaire I2)
'It was too much of a strain. The lessons were too frequent. Once a week was quite enough.' 'I expected it to be difficult as it is much harder taking a set lesson by someone else.' (Questionnaire II)

Instances of negativity, overtly apparent at various times over the whole experimental period, suggest that effective enactment of our programme was inhibited to some extent by this teacher's attitude. We refer, for instance, to: the cutting of some lessons to 10 minutes in length, lateness in starting many of them and frequent discussions with the school nurse during lesson time; requests that the observer should set up the instruments; unwillingness to attend the instrumental demonstration sessions initially provided for the teachers, or the two rehearsals of song accompaniments arranged for them later on; and frequent criticisms of class performance and class behaviour, which in the observer's opinion were generally unwarranted.

Such examples of negativity might be attributed to a combination of factors. In the first place, Teacher 1 not only directed our programme lessons, but (a) took Group 1 in two further music sessions each week (singing on Monday afternoons and the BBC's *Time and Tune* radio programme on Thursday mornings), and (b) played the piano, when required, at any school gatherings (for instance, the weekly hymn singing). We realized, after complaints ('I am feeling the strain. The lessons are too frequent' — Questionnaire I$_2$), that altogether too much 'music' had been requested from this participant, and thus from mid-November onwards Group 1's lessons were reduced to one experimental session per week. (A compromise was made in the case of programme as opposed to non-programme music activities, in order to ensure this teacher's continued participation in our project, and also no further interference to the regular school curriculum.[1])

Besides such complaints of over-demand, consternation was expressed over the observer's presence during the sessions. In comments, Teacher 1 pointed to the additional strain of this situation and suggested it was a disruptive influence on pupil behaviour ('children behave differently when another adult is present' — Questionnaire II). With the reduction in programme lessons, verbal criticism was reduced, but the previous tensions appeared to be replaced by an almost 'forebearing' (the word is used cautiously) frame of mind, as evidenced by a passiveness in the teaching and unconcern over delays.

---

1   Teacher 1's participation was sought despite the negative feelings, because we wished to study our materials in a variety of milieux.

Having said this, we should not now conclude that in every lesson this teacher seemed negative, but simply that negativeness was the prevailing attitude. There were instances throughout the programme when the teaching experience appeared to be enjoyed (for example, when preparing for the Easter concert); and on several occasions the teacher seized upon lesson situations to introduce personal ideas — a reflection, perhaps, of what was possible given a happier attitude.

Lack of confidence was apparent at the start of Teacher 1's participation, uneasiness then being both visibly and verbally expressed. But such obvious uncertainty of manner was not noticed again. On several occasions lesson material was misinterpreted and this sometimes produced a stalemate situation in which teacher flexibility went untapped. These misunderstandings generally resulted from insufficient familiarity with the lesson notes. Although usually each session's material was given to the teachers one lesson in advance, it was apparent that with Teacher 1, at least, very little time was available for lesson study.

Such a situation raises the question of how much time one can expect a teacher to devote to lesson preparation, a point which we will discuss in more detail later. Suffice it to say that Teacher 1 regarded such preparation as particularly time-consuming, and therefore misunderstandings sometimes arose, mainly problems with technical points which were, in fact, explained in the lesson materials. It might be countered, of course, that the writer's notes were perhaps too difficult to understand. This criticism could well be justified at the beginning of our programme when the lesson materials were considerably more detailed than later on; and in fact criticism by the teachers centred upon lessons which were taught early in the programme.[1] But other than this, the teachers agreed that the instruction notes were sufficiently clear.

Although Teacher 1 was the most musically skilled of our participants, there were instances (in terms of our criteria) when the teaching lacked expertise. As before, this could sometimes be traced to unfamiliarity with the lesson notes, but it was the reservedness of this teacher that occasioned most of the criticisms. Since these criticisms in fact highlight

---

1   We refer to Questionnaires I_1 and I_2, respectively, where in answer to the question 'Were the instructions clear enough?', Teacher 3a replied in the negative, and Teacher 3b complained about the complexity of one particular lesson.

some of the problems which a less musically experienced teacher might encounter, we shall discuss such problems and the amendments they necessitated in the next chapter.

In summary, Teacher 1 demonstrated a certain hostility towards the programme which in observations based on our criteria inhibited effective programme enactment. Full exploration of the 'teachability' of our programme was checked by these negative reactions; and thus in the case of this non-specialist, our programme's viability is open to question.

b. *Teacher 2.* Out of 90 lessons given to Group 2, 88 were taught by Teacher 2, and the remaining two lessons by the Deputy Headmaster and Teacher 3a, respectively, when the class teacher was absent.

Based on our observations, and comments from the questionnaires, we surmise that Teacher 2 was an eager participant in our programme:

> 'I enjoy a challenge! My teaching resources did not include music, and anything that would perhaps make me a more interesting and competent teacher is of value.' (Questionnaire II)
> 'I have enjoyed it all so far.' (Questionnaire I_1)
> 'I am very pleased with the results — so are the children.' (Questionnaire I_3)

A positive and enthusiastic attitude was overtly apparent throughout the experimental period, any negative feelings, if they existed, never being shown or expressed. And on the question of observer presence, we were assured that no uneasiness was ever experienced.

A confident, dynamic bearing was the rule with this teacher. In only two lessons did we observe a lack of confidence, and this centred upon a feeling of awkwardness and visible nervousness during the first lesson, and a wariness of the tape recorder during the third. We also noted flexibility in the teaching situation, a personal touch often being added to the presentation of lessons.

It was obvious that the writer's notes were always well studied by Teacher 2. Only a few minor misunderstandings of the lesson material ever arose, and these were mainly during initial sessions. Moreover, the teaching, in general, was highly proficient. So 'in tune' was this teacher with the project's aims and the means of translating and enacting our programme that it was possible to attempt with Group 2 such large-scale items as *Fun for Four Drums* and *The Three Bears* (see Chapter Four), the latter work being learned by the pupils inside two weeks.

In summary, for Teacher 2, the music teaching became a catalyst for dynamic interchanges. Not only were project aims furthered by the nature of the response, but observations, based on our criteria, indicated an effective enactment of our programme. Thus in relation to this nonspecialist our programme appeared to be practicable.

c. *Teacher 3a*. We have noted that during our project, two different teachers were assigned to Group 3, Teacher 3a prior to the Summer vacation and Teacher 3b for the remainder of the experimental period. Out of 96 lessons given to this group, 17 were taught by Teacher 3a (13 lessons initially while in the capacity of regular classroom teacher, and four lessons during the Autumn term while acting as a substitute for Teacher 3b). The first three lessons of the group were taught by the Deputy Headmaster during Teacher 3a's absence.

Our observations, together with comments from the questionnaires, suggest that Teacher 3a, though willing to participate, experienced great anxiety in this participation — at least initially. Lack of confidence was quite apparent in the early stages.

'The lessons started badly and have improved, due I think to [my] confidence being bolstered by success in singing.' '[So far I have found the music teaching] more difficult [than I had expected].' (Questionnaire I$_1$)

Further problems arose in connection with the class itself. Prior to the Summer vacation, Group 3's behaviour was, according to the staff, particularly difficult to control, a situation which seemed to be due mainly to several troublesome pupils who in the Autumn term moved up the school. Teacher 3a was at times necessarily preoccupied with behaviour problems, which only added insult to injury in respect of the music teaching.

It appears that at first this teacher found the music teaching quite difficult, particularly the rhythmical activities and the notation topics. There were misunderstandings and inexpertise in the teaching of these, though we must admit this was at the start of the programme when the teacher's inhibitions and tensions were paramount. In the event, the problems encountered by Teacher 3a led to some amendments in these topics (for instance, a pulse group was added to overcome the teacher's timing problem — see Chapter Seven). With increasing experience, and possibly the amendments to these topics, proficiency began to improve.

Least problems for this teacher seemed to arise from the singing and instrumental accompaniments, topics which appeared to be taught with some enjoyment. As we have noted, Teacher 3a admitted to a growing confidence through success in singing. This growth, which complemented a growing proficiency overall, was reflected in the four lessons which were taught in the Autumn term.

In view of Teacher 3a's response to the music teaching, the need for an orientation programme must be considered. It was apparent that our lesson notes were always carefully and conscientiously studied by this teacher, but more was needed, as Teacher 3a was quick to point out:

'If the teacher and yourself could, as a matter of course, run through the following lesson during a dinner break, or some such time, I think that the instructions would be understood and taught better.'

'Given a lot more practice I feel I could make a reasonable attempt at music teaching.' (Questionnaire I$_2$)

In summary, for Teacher 3a, the music teaching presented a formidable challenge, requiring much guidance and practice on the teacher's part in order to cope. Project aims were, however, furthered by the nature of the response. Moreover, observations *in toto* and based on our criteria, indicated an apparently effective enactment of our programme. In relation to this non-specialist, then, our programme appeared to be practicable.

d. *Teacher 3b*. Out of the 96 lessons given to Group 3, 76 were taught by Teacher 3b. This participant was reluctant at being asked to do music, but nonetheless agreed to the teaching in the interests of the project:

'[I felt] reluctance — but willing [when asked to do music]. Fears of singing to class audience.' 'I did not know what to expect. It was a foreign language all over again.' (Questionnaire II)

Although it was never outwardly apparent, a negative attitude initially existed towards the music: Teacher 3b in fact admitted to at first thinking it was a waste of time doing music with these children. There was also a negative reaction to some of the topics, specifically the rhythmical activities, the notation and the integrative activities.

As time progressed, however, the general negativeness to the project abated and in fact a complete reversal of opinion eventually ensued. By Christmas, Teacher 3b was commenting on the benefits of music for the children — another means of communication, for instance — and was expressing surprise about the group's rapid accomplishments and the fact that music signified so much to them. The notation activities were also viewed more favourably, to the extent that in the final questionnaire this teacher even expressed a desire to complete the notation to FACE and EGBDF level eventually. At the end of the day, Teacher 3b explained this general change in attitude towards our programme:

'I began to enjoy it as much as, if not more than the children. I began to see how it generally helped me in establishing relationships in a creative atmosphere.' '[I have gained] pleasure — confidence to tackle new things.' (Questionnaire II)

And, as regards the benefits of regular music lessons for ESN children:

'Extremely beneficial — gives a lot of confidence to the children.' (Questionnaire II)

Despite initial doubts about the lessons, Teacher 3b always appeared to be full of self-assurance. Dynamic and lively, this teacher led the class expertly, usually managing to involve most of the children and adding spontaneous personal touches to the presentation. We confirm, too, that no uneasiness was experienced over the observer's presence (Questionnaire II).

Even so, the appearance of confidence was not always

indicative of the feeling. As we know, this teacher was a little self-conscious about singing and admitted to experiencing difficulties learning the melodies of unfamiliar songs. In addition, the pitch notation topic was approached very warily.

But such feelings did not seem to detract from the teaching. The few misunderstandings that did arise appeared to result from inadequate familiarity with the lesson notes, which was in fact a point of contention ('restrict necessary preliminary preparation to a minimum' — Questionnaire I2). On the other hand, the dynamic approach of this teacher did not seem to be in keeping with a strict adherence to detailed lesson plans, the writer's materials being looked upon more as a collection of ideas for making music, to be flexibly interpreted according to the moment ('The fact that we did sometimes unexpected things did act as a spur!' — Questionnaire II). Despite such freedoms, there were very few instances when the teaching lacked expertise, and in general no great fault could be found as regards music teaching proficiency.

In summary, for Teacher 3b, the music teaching appeared to be an impotent proposition which in the event bore fruit. Not only were project aims furthered by the nature of the response, but observations, based on our criteria, indicated an apparently effective enactment of our programme. In relation to this non-specialist, therefore, our programme again appeared to be practicable.

Teacher response as revealed in the questionnaires

The teachers' replies to the questionnaires fall roughly into our three categories of analysis, but for clarity in this instance they will be discussed under the following headings: the music teaching, the pupils and the programme. From the statements made by our teachers, inferences can be drawn about their response to the music teaching and their ability to cope in this role. It will be seen that earlier discussed observations are reinforced.

The music teaching. Teacher 1's replies to the questionnaires were in general negative, reflecting the attitude previously described in our observations. We note, for instance, from Questionnaire II that this teacher expected the teaching to be difficult, would not have agreed to the teaching if its demands had been foreseeable, found the teaching burdensome and too much of a strain, felt the lessons were too frequent, and was bothered by the investigator's presence; in fact it was twice proposed that the writer, herself, should take the lessons.

Apart from the above teacher's attitude, the general response in the questionnaires was encouraging. The other participants were at first conscious of doubts and uncertainties as to their capabilities; and the unfamiliarity of the situation prompted initial feelings that the teaching was difficult (we refer to particular problems mentioned in Questionnaire I: learning new and unfamiliar songs, coping with rehearsal techniques, and coping with notation and explanation). With time, however, the teaching was viewed as progressively less difficult, so that by the end of our project, Teachers 2, 3a and 3b could state that they were aware of their growing proficiency and confidence.

Our teachers were unanimous in stating they had gained something from the experience — for example: the ability to help the children gain a wider understanding, a knowledge that it is possible for a teacher to learn along with the children, and recognition that the idea 'teacher's dignity must be maintained at all times' is shortsighted (Teacher 2); confidence to tackle new things, and enjoyment in seeing and hearing what one's class has achieved (Teacher 3b). We find particularly interesting the comment of Teacher 3a, who after a doubtful initial attempt at the music teaching, could foresee being able to cope given more practice.

As we have seen, Teacher 2 viewed the teaching as a challenge and a means to greater competence as a teacher. We note from the questionnaires that neither Teacher 2 nor 3b found the demands of our programme too burdensome; neither teacher was discouraged by the teaching experiences (Teacher 2 commented: 'I was never discouraged, mainly because the children amazed me with their competence and retention of work'); and neither teacher was bothered by the investigator's presence.

Our participants unanimously agreed that the non-specialist teaching of music is a valid proposition. All wished to continue doing some music in the future, the nature of many of their comments suggesting that their planned activities would emanate from ideas in the present programme.

Significantly, for two of our three main participating teachers, and the temporary participant (Teacher 3a), music teaching of the sort specified in our programme proved to be both practicable and worthwhile.

The pupils. Apart from Teacher 1 who felt that our programme lessons were of no benefit to the youngest group, the general feeling expressed by our teachers was that the children both enjoyed and benefited from our music classes; according to the questionnaires, in only three cases did a pupil actually remark that he disliked the lessons (pupils of Teacher 1 and 3a, respectively). Otherwise, the comments denote surprise over the pupils' response, as the following remarks from Teachers 2, 3a and 3b illustrate:

Teacher 3a: 'Children I thought would have no liking or aptitude for music have shown the opposite reaction.' 'I expected much less. I am pleased.' (Questionnaire I$_1$)

Teacher 2: 'Children are really keen to carry on with work.' (Questionnaire I$_2$) 'I am very pleased with the results — so are the children.' (Questionnaire I$_3$) 'I expected them to be shy and perhaps loath to try something new. They have achieved far more than I expected.' (Questionnaire II)

Teacher 3b: 'Very satisfactory results.' (Questionnaire I$_2$) 'Children who are generally reticent have shown eagerness to play an active part. The less academically attuned are making music their *forte*.' (Questionnaire I$_3$) 'They have achieved a great deal of satisfaction and pride in their work and a very good level of musical expertise (notation) and manual dexterity, sense of timing.' (Questionnaire II)

Teacher 2 points to the importance for the children of enjoying a new experience; Teacher 3b points to the Christmas and Easter concerts as evidence of pupil accomplishments. The general feeling in the questionnaires was that there had been improvements in co-ordination, and attention span, and that there was good co-operation amongst the children. Teachers 2 and 3b note instances where the music prompted lethargic pupils and elicited co-operation from aggressive or maladjusted pupils; Teacher 3b makes a particularly interesting point: 'Generally it gave a feeling of 100 per cent class activity as all were at the same level and conscious that it was a skill they had acquired – at Easter concert, for example – which their contemporaries in other schools did not have.' (Questionnaire II) We note with similar interest what this teacher says about carry-over effects – or the influence of successful musical experiences on other lessons: 'Simon – established his competence in one field; now readily accepts challenge in reading! Les – weak reader; now confident of ability to read music and words. Maurice – memory has improved enormously; becoming lively in inquiring manner.' (Questionnaire II)

In general, then, the teachers (apart from Teacher 1) were satisfied and even delighted with the response of their pupils to the music teaching.

The programme. We note from the questionnaires the teachers' initial feeling that there was too much material to cover in a lesson, an opinion which corresponded with the uncertainty and doubts they expressed at the beginning of the teaching. But as the programme progressed, the feeling of over-demand was no longer general (this, despite the fact that our project was a trial endeavour and under pressure of time). As we noted earlier, apart from two instances, the lesson instructions were thought to be clear enough throughout. The teachers also agreed that the children had understood the lessons. The activity at first favoured by the pupils was said to be singing, though with the later emphasis on instrumental work as an accompaniment to the singing, songs with accompaniments became the highlighted activity.

There were mixed opinions as to whether the children were bored with any topic. In some cases, the teachers thought not – for example, Teacher 2 comments: 'Children have been too busy to be bored.' At other times topics were singled out because of their surfeit in the lesson schedule or because they were prolonged by the teacher – specifically, rhythmic imitation, the clapping sequences and the notation exercises. We learn from our teachers that they, themselves, were not bored by any topic, though Teacher 3b would have preferred not to do the integrative activities.

In summative opinions, the teachers agreed that the standards set in the lessons were attainable by the children, although according to Teacher 1, *only by the brighter pupils.* Teacher 2 says of Group 2's response: 'They did not give any indication — i.e. of displeasure at forthcoming lesson, petulance or fear at not being able to cope — that the work was beyond their capabilities.' Likewise, Teacher 3b thought the lesson material corresponded to Group 3's stage of development, 'because my approach to them is similar to "top" juniors and I know from experience that they (juniors) would relish this programme'. The teachers also agreed that the steps in the learning of the skills were presented at a reasonable rate, Teacher 3b pointing out that the children also established their own rate, and Teacher 2 commenting: 'After careful consideration, I think the work has been very well geared for the children.' The only pupil difficulties actually specified by the teachers concerned, firstly, apparent problems with instrumental entries by Group 1 (a difficulty whose resolution largely depends on effective cueing by the teacher), and secondly, some confusion over the naming of notes in one of Group 3's lessons.

For Teacher 2, the first few lessons presented the most teaching problems 'simply because I was not used to this kind of work'. For Teacher 3b, it was the organization of instruments for different songs. For Teacher 3a, problems were encountered with the notation topics and rhythm without melody. Teacher 1 did not comment on this point.

We find various suggestions on lesson planning in the questionnaires. All our teachers agreed that two music lessons per week would probably be the most practicable number for ESN children (Teacher 3b also suggested an extra day every month). Of the individual proposals offered *re* the programme, the following appeared in Questionnaire I: less material per lesson, more singing, taping of the children's performances, restricting of the preliminary lesson preparation to a minimum, and more guidance for the teaching. Content suggestions were made in both questionnaires, including: music and mime, playing excerpts from classical music to identify various instruments, accompanying records of serious and popular music, learning songs from musicals, and listening to songs from the 30s, 40s, 50s, etc. We learn from the final questionnaire that Teacher 2 would have liked more time in the programme for instrumental work and music reading, while Teacher 3b would have liked to develop the Rondo further (see Appendix A, Figure 2). Teacher 2 does however comment: 'I feel that as a programmed series of lessons the work developed, so that in the future new items could be introduced.'

The checklist

Questionnaires I and II were partly concerned with teacher assessments of pupil response. In order to explore more fully amongst the pupils possible non-musical repercussions of doing music (i.e. as distinct from musical achievement), a checklist summarizing non-musical effects was given to our teachers as part of Questionnaire II. As noted earlier, we asked for an assessment of each participating pupil. It was thought that the teachers' everyday contact with the pupils placed them in a special position to make such judgements. General comments on each group appear below.

a. *Group 1.* Again, Teacher 1's negative attitude is reflected. The checklist was returned blank, bar the following comment: 'There has been no noticeable improvement in any aspect except to make one or two dislike music.'

b. *Group 2.* According to Teacher 2, the music had greatest influence on the aspects of mental alertness and memory, 100 per cent of the pupils in Group 2 showing an improvement in these two areas. Of next importance to Teacher 2 is visual perception, which shows an improvement in 95 per cent of the pupils; and auditory perception and co-operation, which show an improvement in 85 per cent of the pupils. Self-confidence and tactile perceptiveness apparently improved in 75 per cent of the cases, motor control and acceptance of responsibility in 70 per cent of the cases, and attention span in 65 per cent. The music had least influence, we are told, in the area of pronunciation or speech, with only 35 per cent of the pupils showing a gain. None of the pupils were singled out as disliking music.

As regards individual profiles, 3 pupils were thought to have improved in every aspect and 10 pupils, in all but one aspect. Least gains were associated with one pupil who was also one of the poorest achievers musically.

c. *Group 3.* According to Teacher 3b, the music had greatest influence on the aspects of co-operation and self-confidence, 100 per cent of the pupils in Group 3 showing an improvement in these two areas. Of next importance to Teacher 3b is visual perception, which shows an improvement in 85 per cent of the pupils; and mental alertness and auditory perception which show an improvement in 80 per cent of the pupils. Memory and attention span apparently improved in 60 per cent of the cases, motor control and tactile perceptiveness in 30 per cent of the cases, and pronunciation or speech and acceptance of responsibility in 25 per cent. None of the pupils were singled out as disliking music.

As regards individual profiles, no pupils were thought to have improved in every aspect, though 2 were in all but one aspect, and 3, in all but two aspects. Striking gains were associated with one pupil in the areas of self-confidence and acceptance of responsibility, as indicated by the teacher's double check-marks. Least gains were shown for another pupil, who was also the most frequently absent child in the entire sample.

Assessment and interpretation of pupil response and achievement

Observations of pupil response

The teachers' ability to cope has been examined in terms of observations made in respect of our teachers during programme enactment. A further criterion of teaching effectiveness and also of programme suitability is pupil response, here examined in order to complement the observations described above under teacher response.

From our observational data, and with reference to the possible range of effects suggested for our programme activities (see, expressive objectives, Chapter Two), the following pupil response categories were determined: (a) attentiveness, (b) response to participation, and (c) reaction to the encounter. In order to define these categories, we selected four levels from Bloom, Krathwohl and Masia's taxonomy of affective objectives (1964), from which we quote:

1. *Willingness to receive* — in the sense that 'at worst, given the opportunity to attend in a field with relatively few competing stimuli, the learner is not actively seeking to avoid it. At best, he is willing to take notice of the phenomenon and give it his attention.'

2. *Acquiescence in responding* — in the sense of compliance without hostility or resistance: 'The more often a student must be told to do something, the more acquiescent is his response, if any.' 'Daydreaming, however, or doing something other than what is required at the moment, indicates lack of acquiescence.' At this stage, suggests Colwell (1970), a pupil will participate in a musical group (e.g. band or chorus) at his teacher's or parents' proposal.

3. *Willingness to respond* — in the sense of capacity for voluntary activity: 'This is not so much a response to outside prompting as it is a voluntary response from choice.' Cues which can be used to appraise this affect include: display of interest, display of co-operative behaviour, exhibition of pupil behaviour in the absence of suggestion and reminder, continuing the activity beyond the minimum requirements, and care in execution. In musical terms, Colwell (1970) points to the responsibilities of group performance, keeping silent when necessary, responding as appropriate, etc.

4. *Satisfaction in response* — in the sense that 'the behaviour is accompanied by a feeling of satisfaction, an emotional response, generally of pleasure, zest, or enjoyment.' Behaviours which can be taken as evidence include: asking for further of the same activities, expressing enjoyment, humming along with the melody, keeping time with the music by moving heads and shoulders or by tapping feet. According to Colwell (1970), the pupil now enjoys music to the extent that he will give up other things in its favour.

Using the above categories as a basis, we charted a profile for each experimental pupil, recording the individual's *prevailing* pattern of observed responses during the whole project period. Each profile was presented in terms of our four main programme topics: rhythmical activities, singing, instrumental activities and notation activities. A rating scale defined the frequency of response as follows:

1 — the usual response, observed on the majority of occasions

2 — a variable pattern of response, sometimes positive, sometimes negative

3 — a response which was rarely, if ever, observed

For each of the four programme topics, we added the individual's response scores to give a total ranging between four and 12; this indicated roughly the quality of pupil response for each activity, i.e. the lower the score in the direction of the minimum of 4, the more responsive in terms of our response categories the pupil appeared to be.

The subjective basis of these scores was readily apparent. No reliable judgement could be made from specific scores. However a *range* of scores would indicate in a general way the response, positive or negative, of the children to particular activities, and to the activities considered overall. The evaluation is thus essentially qualitative and represents an attempt to assess generally the between-subjects and the between-group responses of the experimental sample, Dunbar. Whilst it would have been desirable to get a measure of inter-rater reliability, we note that within the framework of *illuminative evaluation* and bearing in mind both the limits and possibilities set by the *observer* role, we have strived to observe systematically, recognising that the psychometric conventions cannot always be followed to the letter.

Between-subjects response. Assessment was made on the basis of our criteria for an 'unacceptable' within-activity response, namely: a variable response pattern (scale 2) throughout a topic; a pattern which combined variable responses and scale 3 responses; and a response pattern of scale 3 responses throughout.

In terms of our criterion standards a satisfactory response pattern emerged in all three groups. The number of 'unacceptable' pupil responses was minimal in Groups 1 and 2, considerably larger in Group 3 (but with scale 1 responses predominating). There was some variation in the overall response pattern of each group (Group 1 responded least well to the instrumental and notation activities; Group 2 to the singing; Group 3 to the rhythmical activities and singing), though we cannot attach a great deal of significance to this (see the between-group assessment). Insofar as pupil response signals teaching effectiveness, all three teachers appeared to be coping effectively, Teacher 3b rather less so than the others, but overall still far from unsatisfactorily.[1]

Between-group response. Our between-subjects assessment hinted at possible qualitative differences in group responses, but on comparing our groups one with the other, we found no *essential* difference in their response, positive or negative, to any of the activities. The nature of the negative responses also bears on this, for whilst negativeness was variously observed at all our response levels, such responses seemed, on

---

1 In all fairness to the teacher, we should note that of our three experimental groups, Group 3 exhibited the highest incidence of difficult behavioural problems — 8 children with serious personality disturbances (maladjustment, aggressiveness, withdrawal), including one with autistic tendencies, and a ninth child who was epileptic and occasionally took fits. In many cases, therefore, positive responses in this class were more 'spectacular' in quality than in the other classes.

the whole, of such nature as to be general to any programme, inclining to relate more to a particular child's physical, emotional or social characteristics at the time of responding, than to the music sessions *per se*. There appeared to be no pervading dislike of a particular topic such that a pupil was loath to participate.

The reader may have noticed some inconsistency between our previous observations on Teacher 1, and the present assessment in terms of pupil response. Whereas we earlier concluded that our music programme appeared untenable for this teacher, here we confirm Teacher 1's effectiveness. Thus we find a 'confrontation' between evidence, deemed relevant to the overall assessment of our programme, and from two different data sources. Although the attitude of this teacher was basically negative there was apparently no deleterious outcome in terms of pupil response. The reasons for our assessment discrepancy may perhaps lie in: the pedagogical skills of the participating teacher, the time limit imposed on the experimentation (1 year), the reduced number of lessons for Group 1, the age of Group 1's pupils (the youngest group), and the attraction of 'new' activities — all these aspects perhaps tending to minimize any negative influences.

There are one or two further points worth mentioning: firstly Teacher 1's criticism of pupil behaviour. The majority of Group 1's lessons, and in fact after the reduction to weekly sessions in mid-November, *all* their lessons, took place immediately before lunch; in addition, the weekly lessons were always on a Friday. In both instances, a degree of restlessness is perhaps a particularly likely possibility, as in fact Teacher 1 earlier admitted ('lessons on Monday and Wednesday better than Friday when children have been more restless' — Questionnaire I_1). It may well be that Group 1 were less disciplined during our programme than during other lessons, but surely it is arguable whether the behaviour was related more to the music or to the hour; at the same time, we could observe no obvious difference overall in the conduct of Group 1 as compared to Groups 2 and 3.

We find extensive support for our assessments in teacher opinion. As we have seen, the majority view amongst our teachers was that the pupils enjoyed the music sessions, and on the whole responded positively. More point still is given by the many specific comments: *Teacher 2* — '[The music lessons prompted] Kevin, a particularly lethargic child.' '[The music lessons encouraged co-operation from] Stephen, a very disturbed child who could be extremely aggressive. He enjoyed the lessons from the start, was always prepared to participate, made good progress.' *Teacher 3a* — '[Improvements in attention] — Michael, Peter S.' '[Unexpected co-operation] — Peter S., bearing in mind his usual attitude.' *Teacher 3b* — '[The music lessons] gave prompts to Keith and Peter W. Malcolm and Stephen were definitely enjoying their success and have become more ready to try.' 'Peter S., a very maladjusted child, felt important, secure, essential in his role as Glockenspiel expert. Michael [an aggressive boy] liked to show off his good voice, was very willing to work solo.'

It is only Teacher 1 who challenges our assessment by claiming that Group 1 did not enjoy our programme, and if anything, responded negatively to it: 'Most children enjoy singing, playing instruments and taking part in singing games, but for your experiment this was not so. I found it a strain right through as children did not enjoy it, or just showed off.' 'I find the two lessons I take a week (on my own) alright. Children enjoy them.' (Questionnaire II) While the writer is well aware of her own fallibility as an observer, and obviously must admit the possibility of inaccuracies in her observations of both pupil response and pupil achievement, the corroboration given the evidence by Teachers 2, 3a and 3b, appears to give some validity to our observational data. In the light of this support it is perhaps not altogether presumptuous to suggest that the confrontation of evidence arising in respect of Group 1 might be explained, at least partly, in terms of Teacher 1's negative attitude towards the programme teaching generally.

Pupil response as revealed in their questionnaire

We refer to the questions in Appendix G. The magnitude of our pupils' written work in reply to this questionnaire precludes a full presentation of their answers, here. In the following analysis we thus examine pupil opinion generally, allowing for differences in the song repertoire of each group, and the fact that the youngest group managed to complete at the most only 8 of the questions, while the other groups tended to complete 9 (overall there were 10 children who answered fewer questions than these). The majority of the answers were written in ITA, and not always particularly legibly, but fortunately we were able to call on our teachers' help in making the transcriptions.

On the whole, the children answered our questions quite

specifically, making it clear what their feelings were about doing the music. Their comments can be classified into three general areas: (1) attitude towards our programme as a whole, (2) attitude towards specific activities, and (3) opinions about pupil performance.

Question 1, which concerns attitudes towards the programme, was answered by 46 children and these unanimously agreed that they enjoyed participating in our music sessions; thus it would appear that at this point in the programme, i.e. just prior to its termination, there were no general negative feelings against the music.

The majority of questions deal with pupil attitudes towards specific activities, and in this area opinions are more varied. Concerning dislikes (question 3), only 10 children voiced any disapproval — in most cases dislike for a song, though 2 pupils disapproved of the cymbal, another disliked the clapping activities, and another thought that reading music was 'a bit hard'; the other respondents unanimously affirmed that they liked all the music. For question 4, 'Which part do you like best?', there was divided opinion between playing instruments on the one hand and singing on the other; most preferred the instruments, fewer the singing, several mentioned both and one commented, 'I like learning the tune'.

The answers to question 6 varied according to the group; for example, in Group 3 the favourite project song was *New World in the Morning*. The great variety of popular songs named from the home surroundings (question 7) attests to the present-day influence of the communications' media. Only one pupil indicated there were no songs he liked outside school.

The favourite instruments of our pupils were (in order of preference): the Glockenspiel, the drum, the chime bars, the tambourine, the triangle, the xylophone and the cymbal. As for instruments the children would like to play, the piano was the most popular choice, followed by the guitar, and in a number of cases, the organ.

There were only four responses to question 10; one pupil remarked about her preference for the instruments, while another commented on how he liked to make up his own song.

In the third response area, pupil performance, the children named a miscellany of pupils, mostly their friends, as being the 'best' at music; there was an interesting tendency, however, amongst the Group 3 pupils to choose those who were in fact particularly proficient performers. Very few pupils knew anyone else outside their class who could also read music — in most cases it was another participant in our project.

Qualitative assessment of pupils' musical achievement

We shall discuss here four areas of pupil ability which are viewed as further criteria of teaching effectiveness and programme suitability.

1. *The ability to play a musical instrument.* To assess pupil achievement in this area, we chose three response categories from Simpson's taxonomy of psychomotor objectives (reproduced in Colwell, 1970, from which we quote):

a. Physical set — in the sense of correct instrumental position, embouchure, etc.

b. Guided response — in the sense of ability to learn through imitation.

c. Mechanism — in the sense that 'the learned response has become habitual and can be performed with a minimum of thought for the skill process itself.'

We charted a profile for each pupil, recording first the individual's acquaintance with the instruments (i.e. the instruments actually attempted), and then, in terms of each psychomotor objective, the pupil's level of performance proficiency by the end of our project period. We defined as specifically as possible the indicators used to appraise the attainment of physical set and mechanism, for instance: solo cymbal — should be suspended from a hanger, which is held in the spare hand, and the instrument played with a stick which should rebound from the playing surface. The range of instruments we appraised included: drums, tambourine, triangle, Indian bells, solo cymbal, castanets, chime bars, Glockenspiel, xylophone, recorder, melodica, guitar, dulcimers and maracas.

Our results indicate that the instrumental experience of our groups was extensive: the average number of instruments attempted by each child was 4 for Group 1, 5 for Group 2 and 6 for Group 3. In terms of our objectives, the children's overall ability to play their instruments was confirmed, but there was a general tendency towards improvement with age: mechanism was achieved for 74 per cent of Group 1's total of instruments, 81 per cent of Group 2's, and 86 per cent of

Group 3's; guided response was achieved for 88 per cent of Group 1's instruments, 91 per cent of Group 2's and 98 per cent of Group 3's; physical set was achieved for 96 per cent of Group 1's instruments, 93 per cent of Group 2's and 100 per cent of Group 3's. The breakdown of the pattern for physical set is possibly explained by the higher proportion of co-ordination problems observed amongst the Group 2 pupils.

2. *The ability to help make a musical instrument*. All the experimental pupils achieved this objective through their participation in the making of bongo drums (16 drums altogether), each child contributing to at least one of seven steps in the construction procedure. Group 3 attained this objective a second time through their participation in the making of maracas (three sets altogether), each child contributing to at least one of four steps in the construction procedure.

3. *The ability to identify three treble staff pitches*. This ability was tested in Groups 2 and 3, only, using two different pitch notation 'quizzes'; these involved the staff notes g', a', b' and e', g', a' respectively, which the children were to identify in various arrangements of pitch and rhythm. Each 'quiz' was presented on a large-size question sheet placed at the front of the room. The children recorded their answers on paper suitably prepared with the item numbers. The total score possible was 27. Group 2 attempted their 'quiz' on two occasions about 10 days apart; Group 3 on only one occasion.

In our opinion, pupils in both groups showed a satisfactory knowledge of the required work: on the two occasions when Group 2 was tested, approximately one-third scored 100 per cent, while only 2 per cent had scores of 50 per cent or less (the lowest score being 9 out of 27); on the single occasion when Group 3 was tested, approximately one-half scored 100 per cent, while just 2 pupils had scores of 50 per cent or less (the lowest score being 10 out of 27).

4. *The ability to perform instrumental music*. Two aspects were considered here, music which is re-created and music which is improvised. The first aspect is subdivided into (a) rote performance, (b) music reading based on rehearsal, and (c) sightreading. To examine the children's achievements in

these areas, we chose selected performance tasks from the lessons and charted performance proficiency in these tasks for each pupil.

a. We assessed the groups' rote instrumental playing from pupil performance in selected song accompaniments from our programme. The following three-point proficiency scale was used:

> 1 very good, accurate and with certainty
> 2 fair, inconsistent, sometimes uncertain
> 3 poor, inaccuracies in timing and/or notes

The scale level we assigned to a particular pupil represented his proficiency of performance mean in the accompaniment as calculated over a five-lesson observation period devoted to each song.

b. We assessed the groups' rehearsed reading instrumental playing from pupil performance in selected notation topics. For Groups 1 and 3 this involved playing staff-notated examples (i.e. ♩ ♩ ♩ ♩ and ♫ ♩) of the notes e' and g', using the chime bars or soprano Glockenspiel; for Group 2 it involved playing similar staff-notated examples of the notes a' and b', using the same instruments. The following five-point proficiency scale was used in our assessments:

> 1 very good, accurate and with certainty
> 2 good, accurate though hesitant
> 3 fair, with some timing problems
> 4 poor, inaccuracies in timing and notes
> 5 very poor, vague, uncertain

The scale levels we assigned to each pupil were an assessment of the pupil's progress, if any, towards proficiency, as observed during 10 attempts at playing the selected musical examples.

c. We assessed the groups' sightreading proficiency from pupil performance of selected 2- and 3-note tunes. For Groups 1 and 3 the sightreading involved staff-notated tunes using the notes g' and e'; for Group 2, it involved tunes using the notes g', a' and b', actually shortened versions of traditional melodies. The five-point proficiency scale we employed for the rehearsed reading was also used here. Assessments were based on performances during one lesson.

d. Our assessment of the groups' improvisation proficiency was based on Glockenspiel performances during a selected improvisation topic from our programme: see, rhythmic imitation/improvisation, basic topic, Appendix A, part two. The following five-point proficiency scale was used:

1   original, making use of all 3 notes; rhythmically accurate
2   uses only 1 note; rhythmically accurate
3   uses several notes; rhythmical problems
4   uses only 1 note; rhythmical problems
5   vague, uncertain attempt

The scale level we assigned to each pupil was based on performance in the above improvisation topic during one lesson.

e. *Results*. The proficiency scales we used to assess the preceding performance tasks were devised and applied by the writer on the basis of her musical training and experience. Although high skill levels were never expected of the children, and thus the proficiency scales are fairly general, the skill designations do not describe performance in terms of the performer, but rather in terms of the technical execution. Thus 'very good' does not mean 'very good for an ESN child'; it means 'very good from the point of view of performance proficiency', a standard which we would try to apply to anyone observed to perform at a similarly high level of proficiency within a similar musical context.

The variety of musical materials we have used to assess individual performances under each of the headings (rote, rehearsed reading, sightreading and improvising) precludes any detailed comparisons between either pupils or groups. General patterns can be traced, however, as we shall see below.

The instrumental parts for the rote instrumental assessments were fairly demanding for all the classes, increasing only slightly in difficulty with the increasing ages of the pupils. The rehearsed reading and improvising tasks were on a technical par for the three classes, while the sightreading activities were more demanding for Group 2 than for either Groups 1 or 3. In terms of our criteria, to reach level 1 standard in any of the performance tasks, an individual must have displayed, at least 90 per cent of the time, both co-ordination skill and rhythmical accuracy; and in the case of rote performances, rehearsed reading and sightreading, also accuracy of pitch.

Of the four instrumental activities we assessed, the sightreading topic appeared to be the most difficult for all the groups, the proficiency pattern being generally low, throughout: Group 3's sightreading proficiency was slightly better than the other groups', though the material attempted by Group 2 was the most demanding. In rote performances, the proficiency pattern was considered to be good, with over 50 per cent of the total experimental sample achieving level 1 standard (in Group 1, there were 50 per cent at level 1; Group 2, 53 per cent; Group 3, 65 per cent). In the rehearsed reading topic, improvement throughout the sample was generally by one level upwards; again, Group 3's standard was the highest overall. In the improvising activity, the proficiency pattern was considered to be fair, with over a third of the total experimental sample achieving level 1 standard (in Group 1, there were 35 per cent at level 1; Group 2, 32 per cent; Group 3, 35 per cent).

Documentary Sources

a. *Pupil drawings*. The obvious impressibility on the children of their musical involvement with our programme is clearly depicted in their drawings about the lessons. Although we cannot include any of these pictures here, we shall briefly describe four which we thought demonstrated an acute level of awareness on the pupils' part. One picture was a detailed drawing of a Glockenspiel done by a pupil who performed particularly impressively on this instrument during his part in the song *He is Born*. Two other drawings each describe a music lesson: one illustrates a lesson in the hall and includes details of the instrument trolley, piano, and Glockenspiel (placed on a table), the teacher (on the right of the picture) and the observer (sitting in a chair); the other picture illustrates a lesson in class and includes details of a 'Glockenspielist', a 'conductor' on a podium (who apparently is the teacher) and again the observer (sitting in a chair). The last drawing is a pictorial representation of one of the children's songs, *On the Bridge of Avignon*.

b. *Pupil performance on tape*. As part of the Easter concert presented by the experimental children for the rest of the school, Group 2 gave a performance of *The Three Bears*.

Unfortunately the tape recording made at that time was
ruined due to a fault in the machine; since we wished
particularly to secure a recording of Group 2's performance,
arrangements were made with the group's teacher to make a
re-tape after the Easter break. As before, the performance
took place in the hall, but this time without the school
audience; the children sang and played their instruments to
the playback of our previously prepared tape of the piano
and narrator parts. Thus the recording of Group 2's performance was in fact a recording of the children's live execution
of the work as performed to a taped accompaniment. At the
time of taping, this performance was praised by a visiting
expert, distinguished in the field of special music education
(the late P.F.C. Bailey). Our 'captured' evidence directly
reflects both pupil achievement and teacher proficiency, for
the entire performance, apart from the recording of it, was
supervised, directed and conducted by Teacher 2.

Test results

An integral element in our assessment of pupil achievement was our pre- and post-programme comparison of
experimental and contrast groups using our modified version
of Bentley's *Measures of Musical Abilities*. The children in
the contrast school (Hudson) received a music curriculum
which, in our judgement, might be taken as a 'normal' diet
for ESN children in state special schools. The commitment to
carrying through and evaluating our programme implied in
itself a value judgement: we regarded as a reasonable
proposition the hypothesis that our experimental programme
would bring benefits to the children involved. In other words,
we predicted an advantage on post-programme assessment for
the Dunbar sample.

Our test analysis included the following main variables:
five musical ability test scores, i.e. four tests and total score;
sex of the child; age in months; Mental Age; and Reading
Age.

In determining the significance of differences between the
Dunbar and Hudson samples, we adopted *Analysis of
Variance* (Lindquist, 1953), supplemented by 't' tests, as the
main statistical tool. Comparisons were made between
schools, between classes, and between schools and classes in
interaction, on the five musical ability test variables on both
initial testing and retest.

Pearson's *Product-Moment Correlation Coefficients* were

used to assess the relationships between our main descriptive and test variables. Because of the extraneous influence of age on the results (due to matching problems Hudson were significantly older), we attempted to examine the factorial status of our musical ability tests. A substantive age difference between samples could well confound interpretation of retest results, but if evidence could be offered indicating that age and musical ability were factorially distinct, the interpretative dilemma would be reduced. Thus Principal Component analyses, with Varimax rotations of the correlation matrices (Harman, 1967; Kaiser, 1959), were carried out for all subjects combined on retest, for Dunbar and Hudson separately on retest, and for the two schools separately on initial testing (totals on the musical ability tests excluded).

Occasionally 'chi-squared' was used as a check on the success of matching on variables.

Abstracting from our statistical analysis, we uncover three main pieces of evidence:

1. Dunbar and Hudson started out with equivalent musical ability, as tested by our Modified Battery.

2. After Dunbar's year-long exposure to our music programme, the initial non-significant difference in performance between the two samples was found on retest to have changed into a significantly superior performance by the Dunbar children.

3. Although the correlational evidence shows a relationship between Modified Battery scores and Age, musical ability emerged as a separate factor from age in a Varimax analysis.

This evidence suggests that our programme shows promise in extending the abilities of ESN children in perceiving pitch, melody, rhythm and harmony.

Summative evaluation

In the face of our total evidence, the primary aims of our study were clearly achieved. From teacher opinion and *in situ* observations, we confirmed the general practicability of our programme for the musically non-specialist teacher; in the one instance where the programme's viability was questioned, data sources pointed to the experimental situation (specifically observer presence, 'set' lessons and over-demand) as the most probable cause of the teacher's opposition. The views of our participants (both teachers and pupils) and our evidence on pupil response and perhaps most impressively, pupil achievement, attest to the practicability of our programme for the ESN child.

Interpretation of our total data indicates that our general teaching aims were achieved; relative to the programme, our teachers were capable of effective music teaching. Further support is here given to the 'teachability' of our programme.

We have also realized our third aim: to explore the achievement possibilities of ESNs who are taught by the non-specialist. Our results suggest that achievement under such circumstances is indeed possible. And we discovered with interest that our pupils could learn to read music.

Under scrutiny, our Modified Test Battery appears a viable instrument for ESN children, first as an initial measure of general musical ability; and, after programme implementation, as an achievement measure — a measure of a programme's success in extending the abilities of ESNs in perceiving pitch, melody, rhythm and harmony.

From the evidence of our field experiment, we reach this final conclusion: that the class teacher in the special school has the potential to do music, and, given suitable materials, will probably cope most effectively in this role with the ESN group.

Our programme appears to have 'worked' with this experimental sample, but of course, there is the possibility of extraneous influences working in favour of *any* innovation. In the next chapter we shall examine the 'Hawthorne' effect, and we shall look at the problems, principles and cause-effect relationships which emerged from our research, and which suggest application to the business of non-specialist music teaching (for ESNs) generally.

Chapter Seven

General Discussion

'Hawthorne' effect

We refer to the phenomenon discovered by Roethlisberger and Dickson (1939), namely that if one is given special attention, he may be encouraged to achieve. This, then, might work extraneously in favour of new or experimental materials.

The possibility of Hawthorne-type effects arising through knowledge of 'special' participation existed on two levels in our project, i.e. pupil and teacher.

Our experimental pupils were undertaking work which was new and which contrasted with their previous musical activities. In this respect the Hawthorne effect might well be operating. However, we found little indication in fact that the children *were aware* of being special participants. Our programme was given no unusual prominence amongst other school activities (of which there were a wide variety, in any case). Nor were other lessons made to 'fit' round the music; programme lessons took their place in the timetable just like any other lessons.

We note, too, that whilst the presence of an observer was at first a novel aspect, by the same token, it was a consistent aspect, i.e. occurring in every lesson and with the same observer always present, and so became for our children a usual part of the programme. This again lends no reinforcement to any ideas of 'specialness'.

The lack of parental involvement here is likewise worth mentioning. Any information which parents had concerning their children and our programme was gained solely from their children talking about this at home. Our programme was thus viewed as 'low-key', contrasting, for example, with a programme like that for disadvantaged preschool children

(Hodges, *et al.*, 1971), where visitors were constantly 'dropping in', some even working actively with the children.

Obviously the teachers in our project were undertaking new and different work; at the same time, they realized their pupils were undergoing a different type of school experience. There is thus a strong possibility that the Hawthorne effect may be mediated by the experimental teachers who, unlike the children involved, *were well aware* of their own and their pupils' special participation.

Yet, at the time of greatest novelty for our teachers, i.e. the beginning of the programme, when one might have expected enthusiasm to be at its height, the evidence did not support the expectation. Only one teacher (Teacher 2) expressed any enthusiasm at the start. The rest were willing but reluctant participants: Teacher 1 was never enthusiastic, while Teachers 3a and 3b quite apparently *developed* an enthusiasm as their experience of the programme grew. We have seen, too, that there was no obvious difference between the classes in either pupil response or pupil achievement, despite changing teacher attitudes. The only suggestive difference arose in Group 2, who, owing to their teacher's willingness to undergo further pressures, attempted two extended works during our experiment.

At the end of the day, we still recognize that the Hawthorne element may be implicit at minimal levels in our programme. A longer period of follow-up would be necessary, however, to monitor such effects.

Problems associated with our programme

Although the data illuminated in this investigation suggest that our programme achieved some measure of success, we must emphasize that many practical problems arose during experimentation, problems which necessitated a number of revisions to the programme's structure. Whilst these issues are relatively specific, many are relevant to programme development generally, and therefore perhaps worth mentioning. We refer to:

1. An initial inability of Group 1 to cope with rhythms more complex than those involving four claps. This situation was resolved by concentrating on a small number of the easiest rhythms we attempted in the programme, thus allowing adequate time for familiarization.

2. Interrupted progress through frequent changes of

instrumentalists in the same topic. This situation was resolved by allowing each player to stay with one instrumental part for several attempts.

3. Initial difficulties experienced by the teachers in teaching instrumental accompaniments. When accompaniments were first introduced as a teaching task, there was tremendous pressure on the teachers to cope. First, there was the problem of trying to choose as many children as possible to participate instrumentally, and yet still maintain a reasonable standard; but there was the added difficulty that none of the teachers could at first cue the players accurately and at the same time concentrate on the song singing. With experience, however, came proficiency. Each song came to have its associated regular band of instrumentalists who, through repeated attempts at the same parts, began to learn and to assimilate, and so to require less individual attention. Instruments were prepared and distributed more adeptly, and the teachers, generally, began to cope with both the directing *and* the singing.

4. The greatly increased difficulty for the children of coping with three notes in pitch notation as opposed to two. The problem in respect to three pitches was eased by concentrating at such times on the reading of tunes which were only one or two bars long, instead of a whole line of music, and by encouraging the children to work slowly until they were able to grasp both rhythm and pitch in continuity.

5. The difficulties encountered by a substitute teacher in the use of specified rhythms (see 'imitation of rhythms', Appendix A). There were problems in translating the imaged rhythms from songs into clapped patterns, so we suggested that improvised rhythms be used instead. In our project, improvisation proved to be the best method for the rhythmic imitation topic.

6. The tedium associated with singing new songs to *la*. This proved to be a boring and seemingly unnecessary process in the learning situation, and thus the teachers were advised to go directly to the words and melody. This could be particularly effective if the words had been previously reviewed in a reading or writing lesson.

7. Problems in timing entries in the rhythmic imitation and rhythmical speech topics (see Appendix A, part one). To provide an aural reference for our teachers, we incorporated pulse groups in these topics; each player in these was encouraged to chant a one-syllable name with every pulse (or

beat) he played on his instrument. Also, throughout our programme count-ins were considered an essential introduction to all performances, and we therefore issued constant reminders in the lesson notes to encourage the automatic use of the technique; the point we stressed was to count at just the speed one wished the music to continue.

8. The need to adopt a consistent system of musical letter-naming. We have mentioned our use of the Helmholtz system of nomenclature; this identifies note-positions relative to the keyboard through the use of capital and lower-case letters, and apostrophic additions to the same (Helmholtz, 1895; see above, fn. 1, p. 50). On the pitched percussion instruments letter-names are often engraved in capitals only, and so it was found advisable to label the opposite ends of the bars with stickers lettered according to the above system; this could be done once an instrument's range had been established. Our method was meant for the teachers only; for the children, any familiar means of lettering could be used — capitals, lower-case, or ITA symbols.

9. The need to emphasize the purpose of the treble clef in staff notation topics. Confusion arose when this was overlooked. We stated it as a rule that the clef is used solely to point out the g'-line, that there are no other symbols on the treble staff used to point out the other lines, and that all other notes (on lines and in spaces) are found by relating them to the g'-line, after the latter has been identified by the clef.

10. The need to establish the pitch of a song where there was no melodic introduction, or where the performance was unaccompanied. The teachers were encouraged in this case to sound the starting-note of the song, using one of the melodic percussion instruments (hence our naming during our experiment of each song's starting-note along with details of song accompaniments). Occasionally it was advisable to sound more than the first note in order to give a feeling of the key. For instance, this was necessary in *Frère Jacques* (which outlines a major interval in the first two bars) whenever this song followed on from the melody topic (which outlines a minor interval throughout — see Appendix A, part one); in this case the first three notes of the song were sounded.

11. The need to keep musical order amongst the instrumentalists in one particular improvisation topic (see the 'elaboration' of the rhythmic imitation/improvisation topic, Appendix A, part two). Here we encouraged the children to

count to themselves along with the teacher. We also found it helpful to provide them with a visual focus, recording in some way (on the blackboard or on paper) each soloist's entry number(s).

12. The need to save time in teaching accompaniments. In this case we found it useful to copy the details of accompaniments onto the blackboard.

13. The need for careful teacher judgement in assigning parts to the children. Depending on the context, we could sometimes ask one child to perform a melody on his own; at other times we might ask several children to co-operate in performing a tune. An instance of poor instrumental assigning arose during the melody topic in which the instrumental line alternates the notes g' and e' (see again Appendix A, part one); one of our teachers decided to share this line between two children, one to play the g' chime bar and the other to play the e', an arrangement which necessitated one child always playing on the off-beat.

General principles

We hoped that the study of particular programming processes in this investigation would clarify the sorts of problems and barriers that teachers of the ESN, generally, might have in working with the unfamiliar teaching material of music. Part of our study was devoted to probing the music-teaching capabilities of a small number of special-school teachers given a specifically devised music programme to teach. We concluded that the class teacher, though musically non-specialist, might reasonably cope in this area.

In order that implications about the teaching issue might be drawn, our discussion will now turn to the problems, principles and cause-effect relationships which emerged from our research.

The first of our analytical categories — the teachers' ability to cope with the programme teaching — appears to relate to a number of general properties, including the dimensions contingent upon our second and third categories, pupil response and pupil achievements. Whilst there is a close correspondence here with the specific data of our study, these properties suggest application to the business of non-specialist music teaching (for ESNs), generally. We shall thus examine each in turn, with reference to the appurtenant category.

The teachers' ability to cope with music teaching

The capacity of the musically non-specialist teacher to cope with directing the music activities of ESNs appears to be intimately related to the following properties:[1]

1. *The teacher's attitude towards taking music.* This concerns such points as the teacher's personal feelings about such teaching; whether or not the music is viewed as interfering with the usual classroom behaviour; and whether or not the teacher recognizes any value in the music for the pupils. Bruner's point (1966) that teacher attitude can make or break materials was well taken.

The significance of attitude on the non-specialist's response to music teaching is clearly revealed in the data on our experimental teachers: negativeness, enthusiasm, anxiety and a reversal of attitude from negative to positive were amongst the individual reactions we observed, and which in turn affected the way our teachers coped with the programme teaching. It appeared, moreover, that with growing experience and confidence in their music teaching proficiency, the participants generally (apart from the one teacher who sustained a negative attitude), felt happier about their musical participation.

2. *The teacher's attitude towards the amount of teaching time to be given to music in relation to other activities.* The experiences of Teacher 1, in this study, illustrate the problems which can arise from over-demand, which in the event led to the project lessons of Group 1 being reduced from the usual 3 sessions to only one session per week after 3½ months into the programme.

We note with interest that our teachers specified two music sessions per week as the most practicable number for ESN children.

3. *The teacher's perception of how much preparation time is necessary.* Our project demonstrated that this is a very personal matter which varies from one teacher to another. Some of our teachers were willing to do more than others, but in most cases the preparation we requested was con-

---

1 'Cope', here, is taken to mean not only successful teaching, but also relaxed mental set, unbound by feelings of excessive strain.

sidered too much. One teacher expressed an active dislike of such preparation which, in combination with a dynamic teaching approach, resulted in our materials being looked upon flexibly, not in terms of a strict lesson plan but rather as a collection of ideas for making music — as a prod to the teacher's own inventiveness. In another case, the preparation was regarded as too time-consuming, adding further strain to an already strained music teaching involvement; this resulted in obvious lack of preparedness for some of the activities. By the same token, another teacher coped with the preparation without complaint, which perhaps reflects not only a support of project aims, but also exceptional stamina (considering the pressures of the experimental situation).

4. *The flexibility of the teacher.* This concerns such points as the teacher's ability to cope with problems as they arise, the teacher's pedagogical skills and his or her personality.

We continually relied upon the teachers' resource of pedagogical skills during the enactment of our programme. This confidence was often well served when, for instance, circumstances prevented a teacher's adequate preparation of the music lesson; or when a participant with a dynamic teaching approach managed to impress a vigorous personality on the music teaching, thus circumventing strict lesson plans.

Inhibiting effects, on the other hand, were seen as a source of inflexibility. We cite, for example, the personal anxiety initially experienced by one teacher which virtually gripped this participant to the point of undemonstrativeness; or misunderstandings of the lesson material, which often preoccupied a teacher with technical matters, thereby breaking the interactional chain between teacher and pupils.

With growing experience of the music teaching, and growing proficiency, our teachers appeared generally to meet fewer technical problems;[1] and where inhibitions had existed, personalities seemed to come more and more to the foreground — Teacher 3a, most notably. The pedagogical skills of our participants appeared to be summoned in this new teaching task: as experienced teachers, generally, their flexibility tended to become a feature of their music teaching. Terminating data indicate a level of confidence

---

1 The solving of emergent practical problems through continual revisions to our programme hopefully contributed to this.

amongst our participants such that those sympathetic to the project were making proposals as to the content of lessons and were generally offering constructive criticisms about the programme.

5. *The teacher's understanding of the subject matter and proficiency in handling it*. This relates not only to music teaching proficiency, but also to the teacher's preference for particular topics and the aptness of the musical approach we adopted.

We noted in the preceding property that inflexibility, misunderstandings and inexpertise tend to erode interactional relationships and thereby generally to detract from teaching effectiveness. It is therefore essential that any suggestions as to 'music' should be apt for the teachers who are going to do the teaching. We have already discussed the practical problems which arose during enactment of our programme. The solving of these problems, combined with the growing music teaching experience of our teachers, appeared to go a long way towards establishing a standard of music teaching proficiency amongst these participants which, in our opinion, was adequate enough to enable them to interpret and enact the programme successfully. The data in our study which illuminate the category — pupil achievement — bear witness to the teaching standard achieved.

Pupil response and Pupil musical achievements

The latter pupil category appears to be so dependent on the nature of the preceding one that we have combined these two categories in the following discussion of properties. In our earlier analyses, we examined these categories as criteria of teaching effectiveness (as well as of programme suitability); thus, the dimensions which have emerged and which we list below will have some bearing on the teacher category just examined.

The response of the ESN pupil to music and his possible musical achievement seem to be intimately related to the following properties:

1. *The particular musical approach adopted*. This was shown to be an important issue in our discussions about programme content, in comments about the practical problems concerned with the teaching, and in illuminations of the various data (particularly pupil response, pupil achievement

and pupil and teacher opinion). The literature stresses the need for an approach with ESN children which is consistent, structured, simply presented and not overtaxing. The present programme was devised on this basis, with apparently satisfactory results for our pupils.

2. *The particular relationship between pupil and teacher*. In any teaching—learning milieu the interactions between teacher and pupil are multivaried, occurring on many levels of relationship. In the milieux of our study, relationships on the personal level appeared to be constantly changing in respect to teacher expectations of pupil behaviour. We observed that the nature of these momentary relationships could well affect the pupils' responses to the music sessions. To give but one instance, we refer to a number of experimental pupils who tended to sulk if scolded for misbehaving, and when sulking, were usually unwilling to participate in the activity in progress.

Predictably, our different teachers had different interpretations of what constituted acceptable conduct during a lesson.

3. *Whether or not the activity was regarded as non-threatening*. Fear of failure was a particularly inhibiting characteristic of our children. Their cautiousness and often apathy when venturing into anything 'new' was a generally observed feature of their behaviour. For example, when we first introduced the instruments, there was interest shown, but great hesitancy in playing them. In each class the prod seemed to come from the more 'extrovert' pupils — usually the first to be persuaded to try — whose efforts to play appeared then to encourage the others 'to have a go'.

A poignant instance of reaction to threat occurred in the case of one of our pupils who, upon dropping the solo cymbal, burst into tears and for weeks after refused even to go near the instrument. On the other hand, we note the pleasurable response to our musical ability tests (see Chapter Five), and our suggestion that the threat of failure was not readily apparent to the children because they were able to understand the instructions and because they found the actual answering task well within their capabilities.

4. *Whether or not the pupil's confidence had been established from previous successes*. This is viewed as a

corollary of the preceding property. We repeatedly observed during our study that once a pupil had actually experienced 'success' in a musical activity, i.e. actually felt he could cope with it, his willingness to participate (in the sense of our response level 'willingness to respond', see Chapter Six) seemed noticeably greater. While such an outcome might be presupposed in the case of normal children, it is perhaps worth reminding ourselves that these are ESN children. We thus mention the point for the importance it accords music in the ESN child's development. The motivating influence on the pupils of success in our programme is well demonstrated in our teachers' comments on pupil response (see again Chapter Six).

5. *Whether or not there was an element of familiarity in the activity*. This property overlaps with the preceding. In recurrent observations during our investigation we noted that our pupils' growing experience of the programme activities seemed to bolster their confidence and to aid their learning of the content involved (again, we stress these are ESNs). This could occur throughout the class as a whole, for instance when a new song was being learned: there was frequently an initial apathy, the material just did not seem to be 'getting across'. And yet so often when the children were next confronted by the topic, they appeared to grasp the material without difficulty, making one wonder how the process of assimilation had taken place in the interim. It seems that the slower learning pace of these children, coupled with their incipient cautiousness, perhaps demands a 'warming-up' process in their response to any new learning.

6. *The particular nature of the activity*. As with children anywhere, some of our pupils preferred certain parts of the programme; pupil opinion on this point was sampled from a questionnaire.

7. *The particular time of the music class, and the weather*. On fair days, our pupils appeared least restless in the morning, sometimes even lethargic, particularly during the first lesson of the day. But on stormy days restlessness seemed to be intensified: after an indoor playtime because of rain, for instance, or on windy days, the children generally appeared less willing to settle to any activity.

8. *According to the physical condition and social circumstances of the child that day*. For example, the child might be tired, or hungry or have nits. Some of these problems are discussed in Chapter Three.

9. *Whether or not a topic requiring particular concentration by the pupils was prolonged by the teacher*. Notation activities were especially prone to prolongation by our teachers, and pupil fatigue was invariably the result.

10. *According to teacher effectiveness*. This property has already been discussed under the teacher category, above.

A final note. Although we have cited pedagogical skills as an important teaching resource in implementing our programme, these skills are no substitute for an adequate understanding of content in the more involved programme topics. We observed, for instance, that when a teacher had been unable to prepare sufficiently for the pitch notation lessons, i.e. had been unable to do more than a quick read-through of the material, important teaching points could be overlooked, and this in turn could lead to confusion amongst the pupils.

Implications

The properties we have listed above as being generally applicable to non-specialist music teaching (for ESNs) point to the very personal nature of such teaching participation, and the multiplicity of influences affecting both teacher and pupil response. Presumably, each learning milieu will bring a different permutation of the properties to bear on the translation and enactment of a particular programme, and undoubtedly will uncover further related dimensions in the process. It is worth emphasizing that the above properties emerged from a pressured, research-oriented field situation: an observer present at each music session; no orientation programme preceding the teachers' participation; and intensive lesson schedules — three sessions per week per teacher, in the main. Under more favourable conditions, it is perhaps possible that a non-specialist's ability to cope with music with ESNs would be amplified.

The implications to be drawn from our investigation are necessarily very general. The first point we would make is that any ESN music programme of the present sort and intended for teaching by the musically non-specialist teacher, should preferably be organized as a guide which can be borrowed from freely, but structurally, according to the teacher's particular inclinations, i.e. interests, confidence, teaching approach, as well as knowledge of the children, and the school and classroom situation. In this way, the teacher in effect organizes his own music programme.

There are two corollaries to this. Firstly, the pedagogical skills of participating teachers might well be recognized as an *aid* to the music teaching. Brief, but comprehensible explanations would seem to be preferable to detailed programme instructions. And secondly, the use of such a programme guide should entail for the teacher the minimum of pre-lesson preparation.

We believe attention should be paid to the arrangements for music so as to accord as closely as possible with the class teacher's views as to both the amount of time to be devoted to this activity and the specific times of the actual sessions.

Judging by the initial apprehensions experienced by our teachers, an orientation course would seem expedient prior to any musically non-specialist teacher undertaking teaching of this kind. We noted at the beginning of this book that short courses are offered by many local education authorities, as well as advisory visits from LEA music advisers and annual national summer courses organized by the Standing Conference for Amateur Music. We hope, however, that the Guide we present in Appendix A will be sufficiently instructive to allay the non-specialist's apprehensions about taking music with ESN children, and to establish a mental set in concert with the idea of learning along with the pupils.

At the same time, it is as well to realize that a musically inexperienced teacher may legitimately feel a little overwhelmed in the initial stages of this new teaching situation and that feelings of awkwardness, uncertainty and doubtfulness are likely to arise. Hence, a warming-up, probationary period of music teaching should preferably take place before such a teacher decides whether or not he can really cope in this role, or makes any judgements, affirmative or negative, about the value of music for these children.

It would be desirable if our conclusions could be confirmed through replication of the programme teaching. In addition we should be interested to see the following issues examined:

1. Age differentiated responses to various musical activities.

2. Sex differentiated responses to various musical activities.

3. The integration of music into the life of the school.

4. Possibilities for further musical activities.

5. Comparison of specialist and non-specialist music teaching in this area.

6. Extension of the pupils' music reading to FACE and EGBDF level.

7. Possibilities for developing individual instrumental proficiencies amongst the pupils.

8. Possibilities for the use of audio-visual aids.

With this, we end the first part of our book which has looked at our research study in all its aspects. In Appendix A, we present the practical realization of these investigations, our guide to musical activities; and in Appendix D, the notation of and instructions for our musical ability tests.

APPENDIX A

A Guide to Musical Activities

The material we present in this Appendix is regarded as a guide to the sorts of musical activities which can be undertaken with ESN pupils by the musically non-specialist class teacher. The structured series of topics which we include are based on those of our field study, and illustrate what has been done and, by inference, what can be done musically with these children by the non-specialist. If the reader intends to make use of this guide, it is strongly recommended that Chapter Four be studied in conjunction to give a necessary perspective (an outline of the programme is given there in Figure 1). One might also briefly review the practical problems discussed in Chapter Seven.

Our guide offers suggestions. It is expected that the teacher will also experiment with his own choices of material. Indeed, on the basis of our study, we attach great importance to the pedagogical skills of the teachers and their detailed knowledge and experience of teaching ESN children generally. It is hoped that by using our guide as a starting point, a teacher will be able to organize his own music programme according to what he feels confident enough to attempt, his judgement of pupil capabilities, his teaching approach with ESN children, his particular interests, and the school and classroom situation.

Our study has dealt with a teaching task from the viewpoint of its unfamiliarity to those participating in the teaching. In any new task one must expect certain feelings of awkwardness to arise, but in teaching music it is important to make as personal a contribution as possible. Self-consciousness must be masked if one is to make any impact at all through this art-form. The teacher should be a focus of attention for the class: guiding, directing, encouraging, cueing, singing and clapping with the children — in short, *leading* every aspect of the music session, while infused with a spirit of contagious enthusiasm! Music is an expression of emotion — passivity, especially for these children who appear to rely so much on direct and forceful stimulation, is fatal.

Part one – basic sequences

Imitation of rhythms

Summary. Rhythmical interchanges between teacher and class. The teacher claps certain patterns and the children imitate by clapping, slapping knees, beating on instruments (restricted numbers!), etc. 'Solo' responses as well as group might be tried. Also, pupil can be 'teacher' (class and teacher imitate).

The teacher must take care at first not to rush from one rhythm to the next, but rather should take plenty of time between, and repeat the interchange if necessary. It is as well to cue the pupils' imitative attempt. Later the interchange can be more rapid and stimulating.

Rhythms can be improvised or selected beforehand. *Improvised* rhythms should be simple to begin with, involving patterns of two, three or four claps and growing in complexity with the abilities of the class.

Prepared rhythms require no knowledge of notation if taken from well-known songs: select short phrases, sing them to oneself exactly as they are heard in the song, then clap the sung patterns. For example, from 'This old man, he played one, etc.', select the phrase 'this old man', reproduce it in song, then clap the corresponding rhythm. (The singing is meant as a mental aid, not to be revealed to the class. If, on the other hand, a vocal-clapping interchange is desired, each phrase of a song could be sung and its pattern simultaneously clapped, first by the teacher, with immediate imitation of the same phrase by the pupils.)

Unless the teacher is trying to promote 'free expression' the children should be encouraged (1) to keep their instruments quiet until the appropriate time for playing, (2) to listen carefully, whatever the activity, and (3) always to wait for their cue.

Rhythmical speech

Summary. A name-game. The class is divided into two or three groups, each group to chant a different name or word (preferably comprising different numbers of syllables). The teacher 'conducts', bringing in a group by pointing or nodding, and silencing them by holding up a hand. There may be alternation (one group after the other) or combination (at the same time). Instruments can later be added to beat the name-rhythms.

It is advisable to have a trial run with each group, having

them repeat their name-rhythm several times, in response to the teacher's hand signals. The children should understand that once they start their chanting sequence they are to continue, whatever else is going on, until signalled to stop. It is as well to begin the chant for the first group, and to chant with each successive group at their entry. A trial run for the instrumentalists is also advised, and we recommend that they chant simultaneously with their playing. Steadiness is all-important.

Melody

Summary. A two-note tune (alternating the notes g' and e') set to a word sequence. This is sung, and individuals are taught to play the tune on melodic percussion instruments (chime bars, Glockenspiel, etc.). *Example*

AUS—TIN MIN—I AUS—TIN MAX—I VAUX—HALL VI—VA HILL—MAN MINX
g'   e' g' e' g'   e' g' e'   g'   e'   g' e' g'   e'   g'

Once the children have learned the words and can pitch their voices successfully to the two notes when sounded on the chime bars, they are ready to sing the sequence. It is advisable if the teacher first sings the starting-note (sounding it simultaneously), with the children joining in on the pitch — then a signal for silence — give a count-in of 'one, two' at just the tempo one wishes to proceed (the count-in could be sung on the same starting pitch), and cue the class to begin, singing with them.

Developments. Add a clap on the first syllable of each word to provide a pulse. Invite pupils to play the chime bar g' on the first syllable of each word. Invite pupils to play the whole melody on the chime bars (the g' chime bar is placed on the right of the e'). Other instrumentalists can be added on the pulse. Several children might play the melody *together*.

Part two – introduction to notation

Rhythmic notation

The following activities trace the line of development pursued in our experimental lessons. The approach is largely based on the previous melody topic.

1. *Introduction to* ♩ . This is presented as the musical picture for any child with a one-syllable name. Individual notecards illustrating ♩ are needed.

One child can be brought out to demonstrate. The class is led in a chant on that name — clapping and instruments can double the chanting. A card with ♩ is given to the child and explained as his musical picture or note. Then more chanting/clapping/playing, this time 'reading' from the card. This can be repeated for other children with one-syllable names.

Further ideas. The chanting/clapping/playing can be performed as a pulse in time to instrumental music on record or tape. Also, a game: place several illustration cards side-by-side which the children are to 'read' (again chanting and clapping); by varying the row length, the children will gain practice in focusing their attention on the notes, reading from left to right and stopping when they have completed the performing task.

Materials. To illustrate ♩ we used file cards (6″ x 4″ ruled feint); a red self-adhesive disc was attached for the notehead, and the stem was drawn with matching coloured felt pen or crayon.

2. *Handwork: making of* ♩ *cards by the children (one card per child).* The above procedure using file cards is followed. It should be checked that the note stems are ruled on the right side of the noteheads. The children should understand what they are making. A review of the previous topic can follow.

3. *Word-sequences plus* ♩ . An extension of the melody topic (see p. 134). The basic melody topic is reviewed, then the word-sequence is sung through with an added clap on the first syllable of each word; these added claps are equated with the ♩ note, and the card illustrating this note is shown as a reminder.

Developments. Half the word-sequence can be sung through with added claps on first syllables as before, and these four claps can be 'read' from a set of four ♩ cards placed side-by-side; the children have to stop in the right place. The teacher can help by pointing to each card in succession.

The same procedure can be adopted for the *whole* word-sequence (thus eight claps and eight cards).

Instrumentalists can be added to double the clapping (pitchless percussion; chime bar g'), or to play the full melody (alternating g' and e').

4. *Handwork: making of* ♩ ♩ ♩ ♩ *music pages by the children (one page per child).* Using a ruler (placed horizontally), the child marks off dots at two-inch intervals. Red self-adhesive discs are placed over these dots, and a stem is ruled on the right side of each notehead. The words of half the word-sequence (melody topic) are now written beneath the notes. Example:

♩ ♩ ♩ ♩
AUS—TIN MIN—I AUS—TIN MAX—I

It is important to remember that ♩ equates with a clap on the first syllable of each word. A review of the previous topic (developments) can follow.

5. *Introduction to* ♫ . The procedure is the same as for topic 1, above, only this time a child with a two-syllable name is chosen. The musical picture is now two notes, rather than one. Individual note-cards illustrating ♫ are needed. (The teacher will perhaps gather that ♫ is equivalent to ♩ in time intervals.)

Note: We found it advisable to dispense with chanting, clapping or playing in time to recorded music, because of the inherent difficulty of trying to clap twice for every pulse in the music. The equivalent game from topic 1 can, however, be tried.

Materials. File cards for ♫ are prepared using two blue self-adhesive discs for the noteheads, and blue ink (or crayon) for the upper parts; the stems are joined at their tops by a horizontal bar.

6. *Handwork: making of* ♫ *cards by the children (one card per child).* The above procedure using file cards is followed. Again, the placement of stems should be checked (on the right of each notehead), and their joining at the top. The children should understand what they are making. A review of the previous topic can follow.

7. *Word-sequences plus* ♫ . The method duplicates topic 3, above, but this time a clap is added on *every* syllable of *every* word in the word-sequence; these added claps are

equated with the ♫ notes, and the card illustrating these notes is shown as a reminder.

Developments. Half the word-sequence can be sung through with added claps on *all* syllables, and these *eight* claps can be 'read' from a set of four ♫ cards; the children then have to stop in the right place. The teacher can help by pointing to each card in succession.

The same procedure can be adopted for the *whole* word-sequence, but to give a feeling of completeness, the last card is replaced by ♩ (thus, *fifteen* claps are 'read' from a set of seven ♫ cards plus one ♩ card).

Instrumentalists can be added to double the clapping (pitchless percussion), or to play the full melody (alternating g' and e').

8. *Handwork: making of* ♫ ♫ ♫ ♫ *music pages by the children (one page per child).* Using a ruler (placed horizontally), the child marks off dots at two inch intervals. Blue self-adhesive discs are placed over the dots and the stems (drawn on the right side of each notehead) are joined in pairs horizontally at their tops. The words of half the word-sequence (melody topic) are now written beneath the notes. Example:

♫ ♫ ♫ ♫
AUS—TIN MIN—I AUS—TIN MAX—I

It is important to remember that ♫ equates with a two-syllable word. A review of the previous topic (developments) can follow.

9. *Combining* ♩ *and* ♫ . This involves topics 3 and 7 from above, combined. The class is divided into two groups, one to perform ♩ to the word-sequence, the other to perform ♫ . A practice with each group separately is recommended first.

After rote attempts, the developments can be tried; the children should then be encouraged to read their music. Instrumentalists can be added for variety, depending on class proficiency. As usual, a count-in is advisable.

The note-cards for each group can also be arranged in various orders to test the children's ability to perceive the difference between ♩ and ♫ . The whole word-sequence can be sung, or just half — if the whole (i.e. using eight cards), end with ♩ . Again, there are possibilities for instrumentalists.

10. *Topics drawing from work in rhythmic notation.* There are two topics, here, rhythmic imitation with pulse group on drums, and rhythmical speech with pulse group on drums.

In the first, several children are chosen to play the one-beat note (♩) repeatedly (as a steady pulse) until signalled to stop. Over this pulse the teacher improvises a two- or three-clap pattern which she repeats several times in succession; while still clapping she requests the class to join her. (In practice the children usually join in before they are asked.) The sequence can be terminated when desired, then begun again with another rhythm. It is advised that the drummers chant a one-syllable name to themselves as they beat, and that they start the pulse going well before any clapped rhythms are introduced.

The same procedure is followed in the second topic, but this time the rhythmical speech activity is performed over the pulse. The order of entries is important: the chant is begun for the first group and kept going; then the pulse group is added (the pulse group are to beat on the first syllable of the chant word); with both the above groups performing, the remaining chant group is added. Again, the drummers should chant a one-syllable name to themselves as they beat, and once started should not stop until signalled to do so.

Pitch notation

Here we trace a line of development from improvisation and composition activities, which employ a letter-name method of notation, to the introduction of staff notation.

1. *Introduction to* 𝅘𝅥𝅮𝅘𝅥𝅮 ♩ . This formula is basic to all subsequent work in improvisation.

Using a Glockenspiel, the teacher plays the above rhythm once on each of the notes G, D, E and B (or any others which might be preferred), allowing the class to imitate (by clapping or beating the same rhythm) in alternation with the teacher. Example:

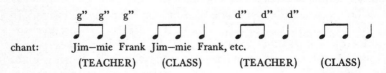

chant: Jim—mie Frank Jim—mie Frank, etc.
            (TEACHER)   (CLASS)   (TEACHER)   (CLASS)

It is desirable to maintain continuity in the progression. The teacher can improvise if preferred.

Developments. The sequence can be extended by adding further notes (e.g. A, C, F, E). The children might clap or beat simultaneously with the teacher (here the teacher should start the chant). If the Glockenspiel is set up with the notes in order of playing rather than in order of the musical scale (so that no change of direction is necessary during performance), some of the children might try the teacher's part while the class chant and clap as before (the soloist should also chant). Pitchless percussion instruments might double the Glockenspiel.

2. *Rhythmic imitation/improvisation.* Basically, this involves the formula  and pre-selected notes e', g' and a'. Children are invited to improvise on the Glockenspiel according to the following formal elements:

a. The 'composition' is to consist of *four* repetitions of the given rhythmic formula, using one pitch per repetition. Example:

(Chanting might accompany the playing)

b. The teacher is to control the attempts by clapping and counting throughout as follows (the class can join in also):
   i. Clap six repetitions of the formula, two as an introduction and four with the child; at the same time,
   ii. Give one count per formula.

Since the introduction expends the first two counts, the child begins to play on count three and continues playing until count six. If possible, his entry should be cued. A schema:

Elaboration. The activity can be extended to twelve repetitions of the rhythmic formula, and other instrumentalists can be added to provide a rhythmic accompaniment for the soloist. Since there are counts, the children can be assigned numbers when they are to play; this will give practice in listening. Any arrangement *re* instruments and playing times can be devised — for example:

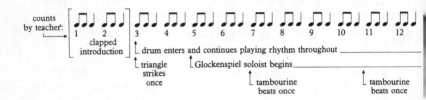

As many of the performers as possible should be cued, but the Glockenspiel soloist's entry is the one to emphasize.

The pentatonic nature of the note combination also allows for duo improvisations, one child at the Glockenspiel and one, perhaps, at the xylophone. It is advisable to use instruments with removable bars, so that only those notes which are needed can be affixed.

Other note combinations based on the pentatonic scale are equally suitable (for example, any from c', d', e', g' or a'). If c', e' and g' are chosen, a bugle call effect will result.

3. *Improvisation/notation.* This involves the basic part of the preceding topic, but the resulting 'composition' is now notated.

Preparation of materials. Two-foot wide sheets of sugar-paper (or similarly thick paper) is needed, enough to accommodate two children per sheet; also blue and red self-adhesive discs. It is advisable to prepare the paper beforehand with the noteheads; 12 per sheet are needed for four repetitions of the pattern BLUE, BLUE, RED — i.e. ♪♪♩ (leave a space between each repetition of the formula, and spaces below the noteheads for adding letter-names and words). *N.B.* No introduction is included in the notation.

Procedure. The basic part of the preceding topic is first worked through. The three Glockenspiel bars which were used are then shown, and attention drawn to the fact that they have letter names. It is explained how we can write down a song we want to keep and remember by copying down these letter names from the bars we play.

A child is chosen whose 'composition' is to be notated. The clapping and counting is now restricted to the introduction, and while the child improvises, the teacher jots down the order of the notes played. (If the means is available, a tape recording can be made.)

The child is helped to repeat his 'composition' and to name the notes he has chosen. One of the prepared sheets (in this case complete with stems) can be put on the board, and the letter names written below the noteheads (see again the first example of topic 2).

The other prepared sheets are given to the rest of the class to complete (stems are drawn on the right sides of the noteheads and the blue notes are joined at the tops; letter-names are then added below). Words can also be invented and added; simply follow the rule of one syllable to one note, and a whole word for every note-block or joined series of notes (including ♩).

When the notation is complete, the 'composer' can play his 'song' from the music while the rest of the class sing the words. As a cue it is advisable to add the clapped introduction (with counts), though this does not appear in the notated music.

Elaboration. A second composition can be notated similarly and the two compositions performed as a duet. Also, one or two rhythmic instruments might accompany the duo (for example, the tambourine on every 'red' note, or the drum on the first of each pair of 'blue' notes).

We found that composers of subsequent compositions were often influenced by first attempts. It is thus advisable to have the child experiment with several different tunes, starting each on a different note.

4. *Melody topic notated.* This comprises two further activities using letter-name notation. The children's handwork sheets, four ♫ 's and four ♩ 's, respectively, are needed.

In the *first* activity, half the word sequence (see again, melody topic, p. 134 above) is sung through with added claps on *all* syllables and a soloist playing the alternating melody; the children 'read' from their ♫ music sheets.

They then write the letter names of the melody (G and E) onto these sheets. Example:

AUS—TIN MIN—I AUS—TIN MAX—I

  g   e   g e g   e   g   e

Various soloists can play the above, reading from the music, while the rest of the class sing. A drum, tambourine and clapping might be added on the first syllables of words.

In the *second* activity, the idea is to add letter names to the ♩ sheets so that this can be played in combination with the preceding. As before, half the word sequence is sung through with added claps on *all* syllables and a soloist playing the melody. Next, a percussion and clapping group are added on the *first* syllables of words, this being equated with the ♩ sheets. Finally the sequence is repeated with all the children reading from the appropriate music sheets (in other words, blue for those playing on every syllable, red for those playing on first syllables).

Letter names are now added to the ♩ sheets. We chose the pitch C for simplicity, but a pentatonic combination allows for D or A also. Example:

AUS—TIN MIN—I AUS—TIN MAX—I

  c   d   a   c

The ♫ and ♩ *tunes* are then combined, the children again reading from the appropriate music sheets (we used soprano and alto Glockenspiels for ♫ and chime bars and xylophone for ♩ , along with the pitchless percussion and clapping). A letter named score of the combined tunes can be prepared to show how the tunes must align if we want to play them together while reading from the music.

5. *The staff notation of g'*. Materials needed: an example of the five staff lines, plus two staff-notated sheets for g', i.e.

(1)   and (2)

It is suggested that the teacher writes four ♩ 's on the board, and asks for volunteers to clap this (with chanting, if desired). Others can then play the same on the Glockenspiel, using the note g'. The children are reminded how we can write down a song using letter names, and the letter name *g* is added beneath each of the notes on the board.

It is then explained that there is another way of writing down music, using a special set of five lines called a 'staff' (show the example). The first of the staff-notated sheets for g' can now be presented. *Relevant points:* the G-note sits across the G-line, the second line counting up; the 𝄞 is a clef (or signpost) which *points out* the G-line by *circling round* it.

Pupils might play this example on the Glockenspiel while reading from the music; the rest of the class can double by clapping (and perhaps chanting). The other staff-notated sheet for g' can then be introduced, and children again asked to play. Finally, the two examples can be played one after the other, beginning with either, and using a variety of melodic instruments. (As always, the children are encouraged to read the music.)

Accompanying using g'. When the staff-notation of g' is understood, this can be written as an accompaniment to the tunes the children compose and notate in the improvisation/notation topics; an appropriate number of staff-notated G's are written out so that they align beneath the tunes — initially it seems best if the accompanying G's are all one-beat notes. A chime bar might be used, and other instruments or hand claps could double on the part.

Handwork using g'. Each child might make two g' notes in staff notation. The teacher is advised to prepare the paper beforehand with five staff lines and a lightly pencilled treble clef. The staff is reviewed and the location on it of the G-note; the children then place two red self-adhesive discs, side-by-side on the G-line (leaving a reasonable space between), rule red stems on the right sides of the noteheads, and trace over the treble clef in black crayon or soft pencil.

6. *The staff notation of a'.* Two staff-notated sheets for a' are needed:

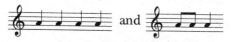

The same procedure is followed as for the previous topic. *Relevant points*: the note A sits in the A-space, the second space counting up; the clef is a signpost which *points out* the G-line and thus helps us to find the A-space which is just above. Equivalent accompanying and handwork activities can provide a further review.

7. *The staff notation of e'*. Again, two staff-notated sheets are needed:

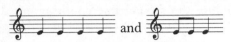

The same procedure is followed as for the previous topics (including the accompanying and handwork activities). *Relevant points:* the E-note sits on the E-line, the first line counting up (or the line below the G-line); the clef points out the G-line and thus helps us to find the E-line.

8. *Sightreading*. Once the children are familiar with the staff notation of two different pitches, sightreading activities can begin. Very brief tunes might be prepared using the pitches g' and a', or g' and e', and combinations of ♩ and ♫ . These might then be performed on the Glockenspiel, chime bars, xylophone, etc.

Technique in this topic is important. A review of rhythmical notation, the staff and the pitch names and their location should proceed, then each tune should be worked through in stages: first rhythm, the children clapping or beating the pattern of the tune and simultaneously chanting appropriate words; then pitch, the notes being named one-by-one in order; and finally the tune, itself, played on one of the melodic percussion. A *slow* and careful approach is required at first; speed will come in time.

9. *The staff notation of b'*. As before, two staff-notated sheets are needed:

The procedure is that of the previous staff notation topics, and includes the equivalent accompanying and handwork activities. *Relevant points:* the B-note sits on the B-line, the third line counting up (or the line above the G-line); the clef points out the G-line and thus helps us to find the B-line.

10. *Sightreading*. At this stage tunes might be introduced based on three pitches (g', a', b' or g', e', a') and our rhythms (♩ and ♫). Suitable materials can now be taken from available sources (see Appendix B): the first note-combination is associated with much elementary music for descant recorder; the second combination is often found in pentatonic compositions. Our teaching technique follows that of the previous sightreading topic.

11. *Pitch notation quiz*. Following on from the previous topic, the children's knowledge of pitch notation might be tested. This requires the preparation of a question sheet in staff notation, using the particular pitches and rhythms familiar to the children, together with suitable answer pages on which they can record clearly the pitch names of the notes identified.

12. *Introduction to* ♩ . Some tunes will require a two-beat note at the ends of phrases; since this is equivalent in duration to two one-beat notes added together (♩ + ♩) the simplest way to present the concept is to use the symbol ♩♩ .[1] Working on the principle of the one-beat note being equated with a one-syllable name, the symbol can be explained as two 'Franks' (or 'Anns' or 'Johns', etc.) holding hands, the tie indicating that the second 'Frank' is silent. Thus, the first note of the pair is clapped audibly while the second one is 'acknowledged' inaudibly by a motion of the still clasped hands; the resulting time-value totals two beats.

13. *Improvisation/notation — staff*. This is a repeat of topics 2 and 3, above, but the resulting 'composition' is now notated on the staff. Paper for this is best prepared beforehand with five lines and lightly pencilled clef. Coloured self-adhesive discs will also be needed.

Elaboration. A longer 'composition' might be tried; or rhythms other than the repeated formula ♫ ♩ . It is advisable to let the children experiment with various rhythms on the three available notes; the rhythm finally selected can

---

1 The writer learned of this method from the late P.F.C. Bailey. See Bailey (1973).

then be carefully reviewed.

14. *Instrumental pieces.* Following on from the sight-reading (topic 10), short instrumental pieces might now be attempted. Again, available sources can provide suitable materials (see Appendix B); if necessary, tunes can be adapted to comply with the particular rhythms and pitches with which the children are familiar. (More ambitious teachers might be able to devise their own tunes.) Various accompaniments can also be added. The teaching technique corresponds to that for the sightreading.

We give here an example of what is possible: we took a Rondo tune by Orff and Keetman (*Music for Children,* Vol. I, Schott), adapted it to the notes g', e' and a', then added improvised solos, ending up finally with a kind of mini-concerto for percussion instruments (see Figure 2).

Part three — songs and accompaniments

Twenty-five different songs were learned in the experimental lessons (see the list in Appendix C). As we noted in Chapter Four, our song teaching approach relied on the use of taped piano accompaniments in conjunction with a breaking-it-down technique. The songs, once learned, were to be a vehicle for instrumental activity and therefore we were later concerned with accompaniments for the children. In the paragraphs to follow we shall look at the question of method in this area more closely.

Supporting harmonies

For the musically inexperienced teacher, the provision of supporting harmonies (i.e. an accompaniment for the voice) can be enormously helpful in both the song-teaching, and the later accompanying efforts of the children. Such supports can be presented in any of several forms — on tape, on record or live:

1. An associate might be willing to provide taped piano accompaniments similar to the type we undertook; these need not be restricted to purely instrumental renditions, but might include a vocalist.

2. Many suitable songs are to be found on record and if desired the teacher could make tapes from these or else use the records as they are. (If the song is to be taught section-by-section the record could be used for straight-

Figure 2: Extension of Rondo to include improvised solos

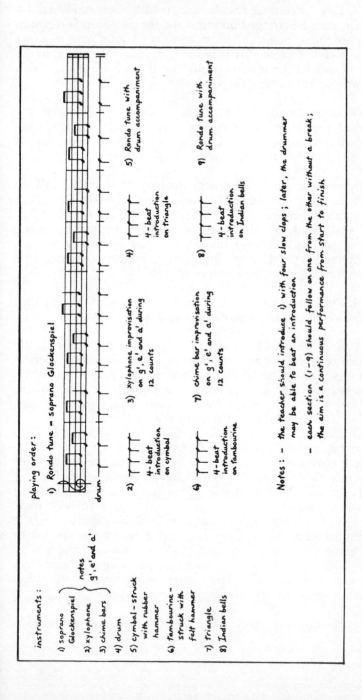

instruments:

1) soprano Glockenspiel
2) xylophone
3) chime bars
4) drum
5) cymbal - struck with rubber hammer
6) tambourine - struck with felt hammer
7) triangle
8) Indian bells

notes
g', e' and a'

playing order:

1) Rondo tune - soprano Glockenspiel

drum

2) 4-beat introduction on cymbal

3) xylophone improvisation on g', e' and a' during 12 counts

4) 4-beat introduction on triangle

5) Rondo tune with drum accompaniment

6) 4-beat introduction on tambourine

7) chime bar improvisation on g', e' and a' during 12 counts

8) 4-beat introduction on Indian bells

9) Rondo tune with drum accompaniment

Notes: — the teacher should introduce 1) with four slow claps; later, the drummer may be able to beat an introduction.

— each section (1-9) should follow on one from the other without a break; the aim is a continuous performance from start to finish through listening.)

3. Live accompaniments are readily accomplished on certain chordal stringed instruments, the autoharp and guitar, in particular; many melody and word editions of songs include chord names for this very purpose. Of course, in the case of guitar, the teacher would need to be acquainted with a few basic chord fingerings.

Whatever supporting medium is used, it is best if the teacher can teach the song by singing it. If our breaking-it-down technique is used, judgement will be necessary to decide just how often to repeat a section.

Considerations in devising accompaniments for the children
There are two kinds of accompaniments to consider, those for pitched percussion instruments, and those for pitchless. We shall look at the uses of these instruments, giving examples from our programme songs (see our list of sources in Appendix C). It is presumed that such accompaniments would be taught to the children by rote.

1. *Pitchless percussion*. These, the simplest instruments for which to devise parts, can be used in several ways:

(a) *As a pulse*. This can be a regular beat in time to the music, recurring either throughout a song or during specific sections. *Examples*. In *He is Born* a child might beat drum pulses (two per bar) during the chorus; in *The British Grenadiers* a child might beat triangle pulses (one per bar, i.e. on first beats) during the third line of text.

(b) *Patterning word-rhythms*. Simple phrases can be out-lined on various percussion instruments. *Examples*. In *The British Grenadiers* a drummer might pattern the phrase 'tow row row row row row'. (The children's knowledge of ♫ and ♩ would also enable them to read this phrase in rhythmic notation: ♫ ♫ | ♩ ♩ .) In *Who Built the Ark?* a child might pattern 'hick-o-ry bark' on the tambourine; in *Waltz Song* the phrase 'und heizt ein' might be patterned on the triangle; in *The Gipsies* the phrase 'tam-bour-ine is sound-ing' might be patterned, as expected, on the tambourine. (The latter word-rhythm furnishes another opportunity for rhythmic notation: ♩ ♩ ♩ ♩ | ♩ ♩ .)

(c) *Highlighting particular words*. Associating certain instruments with certain words adds to the effectiveness of a song. The children can perhaps help in choosing suitable sound-descriptions. *Examples*. In *He is Born* the words 'ding, dong, ding' can be illustrated by three beats on the triangle; in *Turpin Hero* the word 'robbed' can be emphasized by striking the cymbal.

(d) *Exploring different instrumental sounds*. Certain songs suggest the use of different instruments within the same 'family'. *Oranges and Lemons* and *Christmas Bells* are particularly suggestive in this regard. Besides parts for the melodic Glockenspiels and chime bars, there are ample opportunities here to experiment with the pitchless percussion — triangles, cymbals, sleigh bells and Indian bells.

Other songs highlight one particular instrument, for example, the drum in *Charlie Knows How to Beat That Drum*. This song requires the child to improvise an accompaniment which is responsive to the words.

2. *Pitched percussion*. As with the pitchless instruments, there are many accompaniment possibilities for the pitched percussion, but certain factors must be considered before parts can be devised. These are:

Tuning. For these instruments to be used in conjunction with taped or recorded supporting accompaniments, tuning must be coincident. First of all, it is necessary to check that the instruments themselves are tuned precisely (compare all the As, and to be really sure, various other notes also, and keep a record of any differences noticed so that these can be taken into account when devising the children's parts). If good quality instruments are used, no noticeable incongruousness should, in fact, arise.

Next check the supporting harmonies. If a taped piano accompaniment is to be used, compare the piano's As with a common A of the percussion; the piano should be tuned to correspond with the tuning of the majority of these instruments. (Similarly, the tuning of any 'live' supporting medium — for instance, guitar — should correspond with that of the melodic percussion.) If an accompaniment on record is to be used, compare the opening melody notes of the score (played on one of the melodic percussion) with the opening melody notes of the recording. It should be possible to determine whether or not they correspond; if not, it is quite likely that the whole melody on the record *sounds* one note higher or lower than the written pitch — for example, if the starting-note in the score is a G, it may sound as an A on the record. With experience this can be determined, and the children's accompaniments can be devised to correspond with the recorded key.

Knowledge of the key. Songs in uncomplicated keys (i.e. one sharp, one flat, or no sharps or flats) are easiest to cope with, and at the same time permit the full use of diatonic percussion instruments (which are usually more readily available to the teacher than chromatic instruments). Sharp- or flat-signs at the beginning of each line of music indicate not only the key, but also which notes in the song are to be regularly read as sharps or flats; thus sharp-signs positioned on the lines or spaces which denote F and C mean that all notes so-named, whatever their position, will be performed as sharps whenever they occur in the song — similarly for flat-signs (*accidentals*, of course, cancel the effect; the reader is referred to books on the rudiments of music). Obviously, the interpretation of these signs must be borne in mind if the notes they affect are to be used in the children's instrumental accompaniments.

We now consider some possible applications of the pitched percussion:

(a) *Pulse.* This can be furnished by a regularly recurring note or notes to be found perhaps in the bass of the supporting accompaniment, perhaps in the vocal line itself or perhaps weaving a way through both, alternately. *Examples.* In *Waltz Song* the xylophone part might consist of any two G's played simultaneously on the first beats of bars; similarly in *Oranges and Lemons* a first-beat pulse on any D is possible throughout.

Sometimes several different notes might be played *together* as a chordal pulse. In the last mentioned song a drone effect results from the first-beat combining of *G* and *d* in the first and third sections, and *d* and *a* in the middle section. In *The Nightingale* an alternating first-beat drone is possible within each three-bar phrase — bar 1: f plus c'; bar 2: c plus g; bar 3: f plus c' and so on. In *Pass It On* a full chordal effect is possible with the notes G, d and b (or, in an alternative positioning, g, b and d'), played simultaneously on the first and third beats of bars.

With all such pulse accompaniments the emphasis is on regular recurrence and uniformity; a string of ever-changing notes or chords would be difficult to teach by rote, and would present technical problems in the setting-up and distribution of instruments.

(b) *Melodic patterning of particular words and phrases*. The highlighting of certain words melodically can add much colour to a song. *Examples*. In *Who Built the Ark*? the phrase 'No-ah, No-ah' can be highlighted by alternating b' and a' on the soprano Glockenspiel. A more extensive but still simple melodic section can be played in *New World in the Morning*: the phrases 'Ev'ry-bod-y talks a-bout' and 'I my-self don't talk a-bout' alternate the familiar g' and e' notes of our word-sequence (melody) topics and thus would be easily learned. (This familiarity, and the knowledge of ♩ would also enable the children to read this part in staff notation.)

More complicated melodic sections can be attempted if the instruments are set up with their bars in playing order (rather than in order of size) —— for example, in *The Mouse* the chorus words 'up stairs, down stairs' are easily patterned on the Glockenspiel if the instrument's bars are put in the order g', b', d', and f#'. Elsewhere, certain notes in the phrase might well be eliminated. For example, in *The Gipsies* the phrase 'tam-bour-ine is sound-ing' could be highlighted by notes on the first, third and fifth syllables; in *The British Grenadiers* the word 'Al-ex-an-der' might be outlined by three notes rather than four (i.e. f' on the first syllable, a' on the third and g' on the fourth).

(c) *Simplified melody*. Some songs are straightforward enough to permit most of the melody to be played by the children; depending on materials and pupil capabilities, this might involve main notes, complete melodic sections or both. *Example*: In *O I did Climb ā Tree-top*, the first line can be outlined by ascending notes on 'I', 'tree-', 'high-' and 'all'; similarly the third line, by descending notes on 'O', 'they', 'O' and 'they'; in the fourth line, the whole phrase 'I had such a fall' can be outlined during both appearances.

(d) *Pentatonic improvisation*. Some melodies employ a pentatonic combination of notes which can be used in improvised accompaniments. *Examples*. In *Arlequin dans sa boutique* the notes a, b and e' might be selected from a, b, c#' and e' (which comprise an incomplete pentatonic scale of A); similarly in *Hey Jim Along* the notes g', a' and e' might be chosen from g', a', b', d'' and e'' (a complete pentatonic scale of G).

Instrumental considerations

Before we end, a few points about the instruments are worth making. Care in handling is obviously important and the children should be guided in this from the start. A place to store the instruments should be available, and each child might have the responsibility, at some time, for getting them out or putting them away.

The preparation of instruments can be shared by teacher and children. Preparation cards detailing the task involved could be devised so that in a particular song the same child is responsible for preparing the same instrument.

Instruments should be matched with the children's capabilities. A child with poor co-ordination usually finds it very difficult to control the likes of a triangle, and would be more assured of immediate success using a drum or any other instrument with a large striking area. The more difficult instruments might be attempted once confidence is built up.

Playing techniques should be explained to the children and opportunities given them for experimentation. With Glockenspiels, chime bars and xylophones a demonstration is advisable to show how the best sound is produced by letting the stick bounce off the bar; if the beater is held stiffly and left in contact with the instrument after striking, an undesirable damped sound results. More detailed information about instrumental playing techniques can be found in books on the subject (see, e.g., Winters, 1967b).

It is perhaps otiose to state that the teacher should be thoroughly familiar with any instrumental accompaniments before attempting to teach them. This also assumes familiarity with the song. The children's instrumental parts should be explained and demonstrated, and it is advisable to add them to the singing one by one till the ensemble is complete.

The instrumentalists are best grouped together (as are the singers), and if possible placed in the order of their entries; this will make the teacher's cueing task very much easier. It is equally important that children and teacher be able to see each other.

Further activities

We have discussed our other programme activities, i.e. the extended works and the integrative topics, in fair detail in Chapter Four. Since there is nothing more we need really say about these, we shall end our guide here, leaving the rest to the teacher.

APPENDIX B

Sources for the Music Used in Our Project

BRACE, G. (1963) *Something to Sing*. Melody edition. Vol. I. London: Cambridge University Press.

CHESTERMAN, L., and HOUGHTON, W.E. (1953) *Let's Sing: Twenty-four Songs for Juniors*. London: Boosey & Hawkes Co. Ltd.

FISKE, R., and DOBBS, J. P. B. (1962) *Teacher's Manual*. The Oxford School Music Books, Junior Part I. London: Oxford University Press.

JOHNSTON, P. F. (1968) *Children's Singing Games*. London: Bayley & Ferguson Ltd.

KARPELES, M., and HOLST, I. (1961) *Nineteen Songs: From Folk Songs of Europe*. London: Novello and Company Limited.

MAYHEW, K., ROMBAUT, J., and COCKETT, M. (1970) *Moving: Six Action Songs for Children*. Southend-on-Sea: Sacred Heart Publications Ltd.

MENDOZA, A., and RIMMER, J. (1964) *On the Beat: An Introduction to Creative Music-Making for Young Children*. London: Boosey & Hawkes Ltd.

NORDOFF, P. and ROBBINS, C. (1962) *Children's Play-Songs*. Bryn Mawr, Pennsylvania: Theodore Presser Co. (UK distributors, Kalmus.)

NORDOFF, P. and ROBBINS, C. (1968) *The Second Book of Children's Play-Songs*. Bryn Mawr, Pennsylvania: Theodore Presser Co. (UK distributors, Kalmus.)

NORDOFF, P. and ROBBINS, C. (1968) *Fun for Four Drums: A Rhythmic Game for Children with Four Drums, Piano and a Song*. Bryn Mawr, Pennsylvania: Theodore Presser Co. (UK distributors, Kalmus.)

NORDOFF, P. and ROBBINS, C. (1961) *Pif-Paf-Poltrie: A Musical Working-Game for Children Based on Grimm's Fairy Tale*. Bryn Mawr, Pennsylvania: Theodore Presser Co. (UK distributors, Kalmus.)

NORDOFF, P. and ROBBINS, C. (1966) *The Three Bears: A Musical Adventure for an Orchestra and Chorus of Young Children, Story-Teller and Piano*. Bryn Mawr, Pennsylvania: Theodore Presser Co. (UK distributors, Kalmus.)

OFFER, C. K. and DATTAS, J. (1969) *La Ronde des Chansons: French Songs for Children*. London: W. Paxton & Co. Ltd.

ORFF, C. and KEETMAN, G. (n.d.) *Music for Children*. Vol. I: *Pentatonic*. London: Schott & Co. Ltd.

PEARSE, J. and COPLEY, I. A. (1967) *Eight Fun Songs*. London: Chappell & Co. Ltd.

REYNOLDS, G. (1961) *Teacher's Manual*. The Oxford School Music Books, Beginners. London: Oxford University Press.

RICHARDS, H. W. and HOWELL, D. (n.d.) *Fifty Songs for Schools*. London: Associated Board of the Royal Schools of Music.

WHITTAKER, R. (1970) *New World in the Morning*. London: Tembo Music.

WISEMAN, H. and NORTHCOTE, S. (1957) *The Clarendon Books of Singing Games, Book II*. London: Oxford University Press.

The Songs Learned in our Project

Listed below are the 25 songs which were learned by our three groups of experimental children. For full details of the musical sources, which are given here in abbreviated form, the reader is referred to Appendix B.

Group 1

1. 'Charlie Knows How to Beat That Drum.' Source: NORDOFF and ROBBINS, *Children's Play-Songs*, 1962, p. 15.
2. 'Shower and Sunshine.' Source: the writer, 1970, to a poem by Maud Morin (*The Book of a Thousand Poems*, 1959 [London: Evans Brothers Limited], p. 36).
3. 'Oranges and Lemons.' Source: WISEMAN and NORTHCOTE, *The Clarendon Books of Singing Games*, Book II, 1957, p. 24.
4. 'The Nightingale.' Source: MENDOZA and RIMMER, *On the Beat*, 1964, p. 28.
5. 'Out of Doors.' Source: NORDOFF and ROBBINS, *Pif-Paf-Poltrie*, 1961, p. 2. For our project we set new words.
6. 'Rocking.' Source: FISKE and DOBBS, *Teacher's Manual*, 1962, p. 37.
7. 'The Mouse.' Source: PEARSE and COPLEY, *Eight Fun Songs*, 1967, pp. 13-15.

Group 2

1. 'Boney Was a Warrior.' Source: FISKE and DOBBS, *Teacher's Manual*, 1962, p. 82.
2. 'The Wind.' Source: the writer, 1970, to words adapted from a poem by Robert Louis STEVENSON (*The Book of a Thousand Poems*, 1959 [London: Evans Brothers Limited], p. 272).
3. 'O My Little Augustin.' Source: FISKE and DOBBS, *Teacher's Manual*, 1962, p. 187.
4. 'The Gipsies.' Source: CHESTERMAN and HOUGHTON, *Let's Sing*, 1953, pp. 6-7.
5. 'Christmas Bells.' Source: NORDOFF and ROBBINS, *The Second Book of Children's Play-Songs*, 1968, p. 23.
6. 'The Friendly Animals.' Source: NORDOFF and ROBBINS, *The Second Book of Children's Play-Songs*, 1968, p. 22.
7. 'Arlequin dans sa boutique.' Source: OFFER and DATTAS, *La Ronde des Chansons*, 1969, p. 22.
8. 'O I Did Climb a Tree-top.' Source: KARPELES and HOLST, *Nineteen Songs*, 1961, p. 8.

Group 3

1. 'Turn the Glasses Over.' Source: FISKE and DOBBS, *Teacher's Manual*, 1962, pp. 62-63.
2. 'Who Built the Ark?' Source: REYNOLDS, *Teacher's Manual*, 1961, p. 52.

3. 'The British Grenadiers.' Source: RICHARDS and HOWELL, *Fifty Songs for Schools, n.d.*, p. 24.
4. 'On the Bridge of Avignon.' Source: JOHNSTON, *Children's Singing Games*, 1968, p. 22.
5. 'Turpin Hero.' Source: melody from BRACE, *Something to Sing*, Melody Edition, Vol. I, 1963, pp. 4–5; arrangement by the writer, 1970.
6. 'He is Born.' Source: MENDOZA and RIMMER, *On the Beat*, 1964, pp. 32–33.
7. 'Pass It On.' Source: MAYHEW, ROMBAUT and COCKETT, *Moving*, 1970, pp. 7–8.
8. 'New World in the Morning.' Source: WHITTAKER, 1970.
9. 'Hey Jim Along.' Source: REYNOLDS, *Teachers Manual*, 1961, p. 11.
10. 'Waltz Song.' Source: KARPELES and HOLST, *Nineteen Songs*, 1961, p. 11. German text from *Folk Songs of Europe* (London: Novello and Company Limited, 1956), p. 107.

APPENDIX D

The Modified Battery of Musical Ability Tests

The following information concerning the musical ability tests that we prepared for our project, is presented in this Appendix:

1. Notation of the pilot tests.
2. Notation of the tests in their final form.
3. Text of the instructions for the tests (final version).
4. Colour order of the boxes in the test answer books.
5. Example of a test answer page.

A cassette tape of the entire Modified Test Battery can be obtained from the NFER Publishing Company Ltd, 2 Jennings Buildings, Thames Avenue, Windsor, Berks SL4 1QS.

Anyone intending to use these tests would, of course, have to make a set of answer books. We used red and yellow self-adhesive squares to make the actual answer boxes for each item, following the order as at (4) above. For further information, see Chapter Five.

Figure 3: Modified battery, musical ability subtests, pilot version

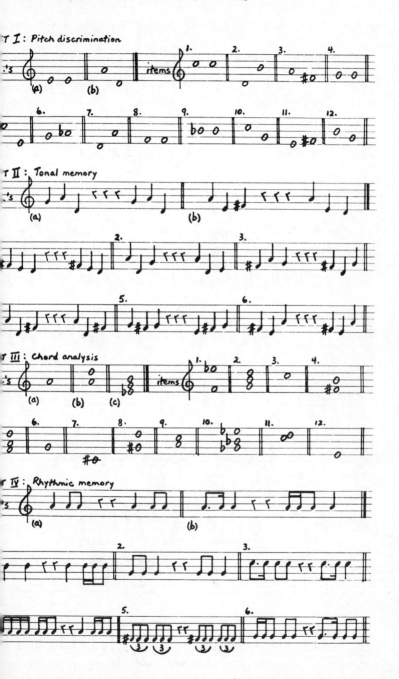

Figure 4: Modified battery, musical ability subtests, final version

Final version of the instructions for the Modified Musical Ability Tests

Test I

Look at your blue book.

This is what you must do for each page:
first, listen while two sounds are played; then, tick one box. Tick the red if the sounds you hear are the same, tick the yellow if the sounds you hear are different.

Let's try one together. Listen to these two sounds. (*Example (a) is played here.*) The second sound is the same as the first, so put a tick in the red box. (*10 second pause.*)

Turn the page and try another. (*7 second pause.*) Listen to these two sounds. (*Example (b) is played here.*) The second sound is different from the first, so put a tick in the yellow box. (*10 second pause.*)

Is it clear? For each page, first listen to the sounds, then tick one box. Tick the red if the sounds you hear are the same, tick the yellow if the sounds you hear are different.

Turn the page. (*7 second pause.*) Here are the two sounds. Listen. (*Item I is played here.*) Now tick your answer. (*10 second pause.*) If the sounds were the same you should have ticked the red, but if the sounds were different you should have ticked the yellow.[1]

Turn the page. (*7 second pause.*) Here are the two sounds. Listen. (*Item 3 is played here.*) Now tick your answer. (*10 second pause.*) [2]

For each page first listen to the sounds, then tick one box. Tick the red if the sounds are the same, tick the yellow if the sounds are different.[3]

Test II

Look at your pink book.

This is what you must do for each page:
first, listen while two tunes are played; then, tick one box. Tick the red if the tunes you hear are the same, tick the yellow if the tunes you hear are different.

Let's try one together. Listen to these two tunes. Here is the first: (*example (a) is played*); here is the second: (*example (a) is played again*). The second tune is the same as

---

1 This paragraph applies to items 1, 2, 5, 8 and 12.
2 This paragraph applies to items 3, 4, 6, 7, 9, 10 and 11.
3 This paragraph is inserted after items 3, 6, 9 and 11.

the first, so put a tick in the red box. (*10 second pause*.)

Turn the page and try another. (*7 second pause*.) Listen to these two tunes. Here is the first: (*example (b)1 is played*); here is the second: (*example (b)2 is played*). The second tune is different from the first, so put a tick in the yellow box. (*10 second pause*.)

Is it clear? For each page, first listen to the tunes, then tick one box. Tick the red if the tunes you hear are the same, tick the yellow if the tunes you hear are different.

Turn the page. (*7 second pause*.) Listen to these two tunes. Here is the first: (*item 1(a) is played*); here is the second: (*item 1(b) is played*). Now tick your answer. (*10 second pause*.) If the tunes were the same you should have ticked the red, but if the tunes were different you should have ticked the yellow.[1]

Turn the page. (*7 second pause*.) Listen to these two tunes. Here is the first: (*item 2 is played*); here is the second: (*item 2 is played again*). Now tick your answer. (*10 second pause*.)[2]

Remember, tick the red if the tunes are the same, tick the yellow if the tunes are different. [3]

Test III

Look at your green book.

This is what you must do for each page:
first, listen while some sounds are played; then, tick one box. Tick the red if you hear only one sound played alone, tick the yellow if you hear two or three sounds played together.

Let's try one. Listen to this. (*Example (a) is played here*.) Only one sound was played alone, so put a tick in the red box. (*10 second pause*.)

Turn the page and try another. (*7 second pause*.) Listen. (*Example (b) is played here*.) This time two sounds were played together, so put a tick in the yellow box. (*10 second pause*.)

Listen again to the two sounds played together. (*Example (b) is played again*.) Now listen to the same two sounds, but this time played separately. (*The two notes of example (b) are played consecutively*.) And again, listen to the same two sounds played together. (*Example (b) is played again*.) Because there were two sounds played together, and not one sound played alone, you should have ticked the yellow box.

Turn the page and try another. (*7 second pause*.) Listen.

---

1   This paragraph applies to items 1 and 6.
2   This paragraph applies to items 2, 3, 4 and 5.
3   This paragraph is inserted after items 2 and 4.

(*Example (c) is played here*). This time three sounds were played together, so put a tick in the yellow box. (*10 second pause*.)

Listen again to the three sounds played together. (*Example (c) is played again*.) Now listen to the same three sounds, but this time played separately. (*The three notes of example (c) are played consecutively*.) And again, listen to the same three sounds played together. (*Example (c) is played again*.) Because there were three sounds played together, and not one sound played alone, you should have ticked the yellow box.

Is it clear? For each page, first listen to what is played, then tick one box. Tick the red if you hear only one sound played alone, tick the yellow if you hear two or three sounds played together.

Turn the page. (*7 second pause*.) Listen. (*Item 1 is played here*.) Now tick your answer. (*10 second pause*.) If you heard only one sound played alone, you should have ticked the red, but if you heard two or three sounds played together, you should have ticked the yellow.[1]

Turn the page. (*7 second pause*.) Listen. (*Item 3 is played here*.) Now tick your answer. (*10 second pause*.)[2]

For each page first listen to what is played, then tick one box. Tick the red if you hear only one sound played alone, tick the yellow if you hear two or three sounds played together.[3]

Test IV

Look at your yellow book.

This is what you must do for each page:

first, listen while two patterns are played; then, tick one box. Tick the red if the patterns you hear are the same, tick the yellow if the patterns you hear are different.

Let's try one together. Listen to these two patterns. Here is the first: (*example (a) is played*); here is the second: (*example (a) is played again*.) The second pattern is the same as the first, so put a tick in the red box. (*10 second pause*.)

Turn the page and try another. (*7 second pause*.) Listen to these two patterns. Here is the first: (*example (b)I is played*); here is the second: (*example (b)2 is played*.) The second pattern is different from the first, so put a tick in the yellow box. (*10 second pause*.)

---

1 This paragraph applies to items 1, 4, 7 and 10.
2 This paragraph applies to items 3, 6 and 9.
3 This paragraph is inserted after items 2, 5 and 8.

Is it clear? For each page, first listen to the patterns, then tick one box. Tick the red if the patterns you hear are the same, tick the yellow if the patterns you hear are different.

Turn the page. (*7 second pause.*) Listen to these two patterns. Here is the first: (*item 1(a) is played*); here is the second: (*item 1(b) is played.*) Now tick your answer. (*10 second pause.*) If the patterns were the same you should have ticked the red, but if the patterns were different you should have ticked the yellow.[1]

Turn the page. (*7 second pause.*) Listen to these two patterns. Here is the first: (*item 2 is played*); here is the second: (*item 2 is played again.*) Now tick your answer. (*10 second pause.*)[2]

Remember, tick the red if the patterns are the same, tick the yellow if the patterns are different.[3]

Colour order of the boxes in the test answer books

Test I, blue book, 14 pages:
   Page 1——yellow, red; page 2——red, yellow; page 3——red, yellow; page 4——yellow, red; page 5——red, yellow; page 6——red, yellow; page 7——yellow, red; page 8——yellow, red; page 9——red, yellow; page 10——yellow, red; page 11——red, yellow; page 12——yellow, red; page 13—— yellow, red; page 14——red, yellow.

Test II, pink book, 8 pages:
   Page 1——yellow, red; page 2——red, yellow; page 3——red, yellow; page 4——yellow, red; page 5——red, yellow; page 6——red, yellow; page 7——yellow, red; page 8——yellow, red.

Test III, green book, 13 pages:
   Page 1——red, yellow; page 2——yellow, red; page 3——red, yellow; page 4——red, yellow; page 5——yellow, red; page 6——red, yellow; page 7——red, yellow; page 8——yellow, red; page 9——yellow, red; page 10——red, yellow; page 11——yellow, red; page 12——red, yellow; page 13—— yellow, red.

Test IV, yellow book, 8 pages:
   Page 1——yellow, red; page 2——yellow, red; page 3——red, yellow; page 4——yellow, red; page 5——red, yellow; page 6——red, yellow; page 7——yellow, red; page 8——yellow, red.

1   This paragraph applies to items 1 and 6.
2   This paragraph applies to items 2, 3, 4 and 5.
3   This paragraph is inserted after items 2 and 4.

Figure 5: Examples of a test answer page

Figure 6 : Format for our observation sheets

DATE
GROUP   Absentees:
TEACHER

I Class reactions:	topic	topic	II. Teacher: *difficulties in:*	topic	*which instructions*
signs of:					
1. attention	—	—	1. — understanding the instructions		
2. inattention	—	—			
3. interest	—	—			
4. indifference	—	—			
5. fatigue	—	—	2. — communicating the instructions		
6. rejection	—	—			
7. pleasure	—	—	3. — getting co-operation		
8. restlessness	—	—			
9. unco-operative-ness	—	—			

III. Individual observations re the instruments — names of children performing and the instruments used:

topic	*child*	*instrument*	*difficulties in:*		*response*
			understanding the task	co-ordinating (specify)	

IV. Trouble-makers:

V. Topics covered:
— all
— in part; specify which:

VI. Personal remarks:
1. Are you satisfied with the response?
   — or disappointed? — why?
2. Do you feel that any progress is being made? — In which topic particularly?

The Questionnaires for Our Teachers

Questionnaire I
1. Have you found the teaching of music, so far, more or less difficult than you had expected?

   a) What aspect of the programme presented the most problems for you?
   b) Were the instructions clear enough?
   c) What, if anything, have you enjoyed doing most?
   d) Do you feel that there was too much material to cover in a lesson?

2. Do you think that the children have benefited from the experience?
   a) Do they enjoy the music classes?
      (1) Which topic do you think they prefer?
      (2) Has any child told you that he dislikes the music lessons? Who?
   b) Have you noticed any unexpected responses?
      (1) Have there been improvements in co-ordination? Which children in particular?
      (2) Improvements in attention span? Which children in particular?
      (3) Unexpected co-operation? Which children in particular?
   c) Do you think the children have understood the lessons?
   d) Were they bored with any topic? Which?
   e) Do you feel they are accomplishing anything?

3. Do you think that *you* have gained anything from the experience? Are you pleased with the results or did you expect more from the children?

4. Suggestions for improvement of the programme.

5. Any further comments.

Questionnaire II

Part A.
   1. Why did you volunteer to participate in the project?

(For teacher 3b, who began teaching after the Summer vacation, the question was worded as follows: What were your initial feelings on being asked to do music?)

2. What did you expect the music teaching would entail?

3. If you could have known beforehand what the programme was to be like, would you still have wished to participate? (For teacher 3b the question was worded as follows: If you could have known beforehand what the programme was to be like, how would you have reacted to doing the music?)

Did you find this teaching burdensome? In what way?

4. When were you discouraged? Why?

5. Were you aware of a growing proficiency and confidence in your teaching?

Did this affect your feelings about the lessons? In what way?

6. Were you bothered by my presence? In what way?

7. Do you think that given a programme to follow — needless to say, one more polished than that with which you were confronted — the non-specialist teaching of music is a valid proposition?

8. Have you any desire to continue doing music in the future? If so, what would this entail?

9. What, if anything, have you gained from this experience?

Part B.

1. In your view, of what benefit, if any, are regular music lessons to ESN youngsters?

2. Have there been any instances in which you can attribute success in other lessons to success in music? If so, please name the child and the circumstances.

3. Have the music lessons awakened a desire to participate or provoked a physical or emotional response in an otherwise withdrawn, detached, shy, or lethargic child? If so, please name the child and the circumstances.

4. Have the music lessons encouraged a desire to co-operate on the part of an aggressive or emotional child? If so, please name the child and the circumstances.

5. What did you expect of the children? Have they achieved less, as much as, or more than you expected?

Part C.

1. Were the lessons too frequent for you, personally? For your pupils?

In your opinion how much time, if any, per week could be advantageously spent on regular music lessons of the type we have been doing?

2. Overall, do you think there was too much material to cover in the lessons?

If so, was this view more strongly held at the beginning of the programme rather than later?

3. Do you believe that the standards set were attainable by the children?

a) Was the lesson material suitable for the ESN? Did it correspond to their actual stage of development? Please elaborate.

b) Was there any aspect which they found difficult to understand? Please elaborate.

c) In your view were the steps in the learning of the activities presented at a reasonable rate so that some measure of success was possible? Please elaborate.

d) Were the musical experiences varied enough?

4. What aspect of the programme presented the most problems for you?

5. Did you find any topic boring? Which?

6. Did you wish to devote more lessons to any topic? Please specify.

7. Was there anything you would have liked to have done that was not part of the programme? Please specify.

APPENDIX G

The Questionnaire for Our Pupils

Questionnaire

1. Do you enjoy doing music in class?
2. Who do you think is the best at music?
3. What part don't you like doing in music?
4. Which part do you like best?
5. Do you know anyone else outside your class who can also read music like you?
6. Which is your favourite song in school?
7. What is your favourite song at home?
8. What instrument do you like playing best at school?
9. What instrument would you like to be able to play?
10. What would you like to do in music in school in future?

BIBLIOGRAPHY

ALSTON, P. M. (1972) 'Creativity in Music: An Exploration of the Relationship Between Musical Divergence, General Divergence and Aesthetic Preference'. MEd dissertation, University of Liverpool.

ALVIN, J. (1965) *Music for the Handicapped Child*. London: OUP.

ALVIN, J. (1966) *Music Therapy*. London: John Baker.

ALVIN, J. (1971) 'My Experiments in Tokyo', *Brit. J. Music Therapy*, 2, 2, 3–20.

BAILEY, P. (1973) *They Can Make Music*. London: OUP.

BENTLEY, A. (1963) 'A Study of Some Aspects of Musical Ability Amongst Young Children, Including Those Unable to Sing in Tune'. PhD dissertation, University of Reading.

BENTLEY, A. (1966a) *Measures of Musical Abilities*. London: Harrap.

BENTLEY, A. (1966b) *Musical Ability in Children and its Measurement*. London: Harrap.

BEREITER, C. and ENGELMANN, S. (1966) *Teaching Disadvantaged Children in the Preschool*. Englewood Cliffs, New Jersey: Prentice-Hall.

BEREL, M. (ed.) (1969) *Bibliography on Music Therapy*. New York: United Cerebral Palsy Associations of New York State.

BIRCH, H. G. (ed.) (1964) *Brain Damage in Children: The Biological and Social Aspects*. Baltimore: Williams & Wilkins.

BLOCKSIDGE, K. M. (1957) *Making Musical Apparatus and Instruments: For Use in Nursery and Infant Schools*. Pamphlet 71. London: Nursery School Association of Great Britain and Northern Ireland.

BLOCKSIDGE, K. M. (1962) 'How to Use Melodic Percussion Instruments.' Pamphlet 74. London: Nursery School Association of Great Britain and Northern Ireland.

BLOOM, B. S. *et al.* (ed.) (1956) *Taxonomy of Educational Objectives, Handbook I: Cognitive Domain*. London: Longmans.

BLOOM, B. S., KRATHWOHL, D. R. and MASIA, B.B. (1964) *Taxonomy of Educational Objectives, Handbook II: Affective Domain*. New York: David McKay Company.

BLYTH, W. A. L. *et al.* (1972) *Schools Council Project — History, Geography and Social Science 8–13: An Interim Statement*. Liverpool: Schools Council Publications.

BRIGGS, G. A. (1951) *Pianos, Pianists and Sonics*. Bradford, Yorks.: Wharfedale Wireless Works.

BRIGGS, G. A. (1967) *About Your Hearing*. Bradford, Yorks.: Rank Wharfedale Limited.

BRUNER, J. S. (1966) *Toward a Theory of Instruction*. New York: W. W. Norton.

BUKER, G. N. (1966) 'A Study of the Ability of the Educable Mentally Retarded to Learn Basic Music Rhythm Reading Through the Use of a Specific, Structured Classroom Procedure.' EdD dissertation, University of Oregon.

CAREY, M. A. (1958) 'Music for the Educable Mentally Retarded'. EdD dissertation, Pennsylvania State University.

CARLSON, B. W. and GINGLEND, D. R. (1961) *Play Activities for the Retarded Child: How to Help Him Grow and Learn Through Music, Games, Handicraft, and Other Play Activities*. London: Cassell.

CHRIST, W. B. (1953) 'The Reading of Rhythm Notation Approached Experimentally According to Techniques and Principles of Word Reading.' PhD dissertation, Indiana University.

CLARKE, A. D. B. (1969) *Recent Advances in the Study of Subnormality*. 2nd ed. London: Nat. Assoc. for Mental Health.

CLEUGH, M. F. (1968) *The Slow Learner: Some Educational Principles and Policies*. 2nd ed. London: Methuen.

CLEUGH, M. F., (ed.) (1961) *Teaching the Slow Learner in the Special School*. London: Methuen.

COLWELL, R. (1970) *The Evaluation of Music Teaching and Learning*. Contemporary Perspectives in Music Education Series. Englewood Cliffs, New Jersey: Prentice-Hall.

CONNOR, F. P. and TALBOT, M. E. (1964) *An Experimental Curriculum for Young Mentally Retarded Children*. Teachers College Columbia University Series in Special Education. New York: Bureau of Publications.

DAVIES, J. B. (1971) 'New Tests of Musical Aptitude,' *Br. J. Psychol.*, **62**, 4, 557–65.

DEPARTMENT OF EDUCATION AND SCIENCE (1964). *Slow Learners at School*. Pamphlet No. 46. London: HMSO.

DEPARTMENT OF EDUCATION AND SCIENCE. (1969a) *Music in Schools*. Pamphlet No. 27. London: HMSO.

DEPARTMENT OF EDUCATION AND SCIENCE. (1969b) *List of Special Schools for Handicapped Pupils in England and Wales*. List 42. London: HMSO.

DICKINSON, P. (1974) 'An exploratory investigation into classroom teachers' direction of music activities, using a specific programme, with ESN children.' 2 vols. PhD dissertation, University of Liverpool.

DOBBS, J. P. B. (1966) *The Slow Learner and Music: A Handbook for Teachers*. London: OUP.

DOUGLAS, J. W. B. (1967) *The Home and the School: A Study of Ability and Attainment in the Primary School*. London: Panther Books.

DREVER, J. (1964) *A Dictionary of Psychology*. Rev. by H. Wallerstein. Harmondsworth: Penguin Books.

EISNER, E. W. (Autumn 1967a) 'Educational Objectives: Help or Hindrance?' *School Review*, 75, 250–60.

EISNER, E. W. (Autumn 1967b) 'A Response to My Critics', *School Review*, 75, 277–82.

EISNER, E. W. (1969a) 'Instructional and Expressive Educational Objectives: Their Formulation and Use in Curriculum'. In POPHAM, J. W. *et al. Instructional Objectives*. AERA Monograph Series on Curriculum Evaluation No. 3. Chicago: Rand McNally.

EISNER, E. W. (1969b) 'Epilogue'. In: POPHAM, J. W. *et al. Instructional Objectives*. AERA Monograph Series on Curriculum Evaluation No. 3. Chicago: Rand McNally.

ELLINGHAM, M. (1966) 'Musical Ability in Children'. Cert Ed dissertation, Kesteven College of Education.

ERICKSON, E. E. (1970) 'Teaching Music to Educable Mentally Retarded Children in Colorado'. EdD dissertation, University of Northern Colorado.

GILMAN, L. and PAPERTE, F. (1952) 'Music as a Psychotherapeutic Agent'. In: CAPURSO, A., *et al. Music and Your Emotions: A Practical Guide to Music Selections Associated with Desired Emotional Responses*. New York: Liveright Publishing Corporation.

GINGLEND, D. R. and STILES, W. E. (1965) *Music Activities for Retarded Children: A Handbook for Teachers and Parents*. New York: Abingdon Press.

GLASER, B. G. (1969) 'The Constant Comparative Method of Qualitative Analysis'. In McCALL, G. J., and SIMMONS, J. L. (eds) *Issues in Participant Observation: A Text and Reader*. Reading, Mass.: Addison—Wesley.

GOLDSTEIN, H. and SEIGLE. D. M. (*n.d.*) *The Illinois Plan for Special Education of Exceptional Children: A Curriculum Guide for Teachers of the Educable Mentally Handicapped*. Danville, Illinois: Interstate Printers & Publishers.

GRAHAM, R. M. (April 1972) 'Seven Million Plus Need Special Attention: Who Are They?' *Music Educators Journal*, 58, 22—25+.

HANDICAPPED PUPILS AND SPECIAL SCHOOLS REGULATIONS, 1959. S.I. No. 365. London: HMSO.

HARMAN, H. H. (1967) *Modern Factor Analysis*. 2nd ed. rev. Chicago: University of Chicago Press.

HELMHOLTZ, H. L. F. (1895) *On the Sensations of Tone: As a Physiological Basis for the Theory of Music*. 3rd ed. Trans. by A. J. Ellis. London: Longmans, Green & Co.

HICKMAN, A. T. (1968) 'Musical Imaging and Concept Formation in School Children'. PhD dissertation, University of Manchester.

HODGES, W. L. *et al.* (1971) *Diagnostic Teaching for Preschool Children*. Arlington, Virginia: Council for Exceptional Children.

HOLMSTRÖM, L- G. (1963) *Musicality and Prognosis: Some Factors Related to Success in School Music Situations*. Uppsala, Sweden: Svenska Bokförlaget/ Norstedts.

INSTITUTE FOR RESEARCH INTO MENTAL RETARDATION. (1973) *Music for the Mentally Handicapped: A Select Bibliography*. London: Institute for Research into Mental Retardation Library.

JACKSON, P. W. (1968) *Life in Classrooms*. New York: Holt, Rinehart and Winston.

JACKSON, P. W. and BELFORD, E. (Autumn 1965) 'Educational Objectives and the Joys of Teaching', *School Review*, 73, 267—91.

JACKSON, S. (1969) *Special Education in England and Wales*. 2nd ed. London: OUP.

JACOBS, A. (1968) *A New Dictionary of Music*. Harmondsworth: Penguin Books.

KAISER, H. F. (1959) 'Computer Program for Varimax Rotation in Factor Analysis', *Educ. Psychol. Meas.*, 19, 3, 413—20.

KERSHAW, J. D. (1966) *Handicapped Children*. 2nd ed. London: William Heinemann Medical Books.

LANGER, S. K. (1953) *Feeling and Form: A Theory of Art Developed from 'Philosophy in a New Key'*. London: Routledge and Kegan Paul.

LEHMAN, P. R. (1968) *Tests and Measurements in Music*. Foundations of Music Education Series. Englewood Cliffs, New Jersey: Prentice-Hall.

LEVIN, H. D. and LEVIN, G. M. (April 1972) 'The Trainable Mentally Retarded: Instrumental Music, A Great Ally in Promoting Self-Image', *Music Educators Journal*, 58, 31–34.

LINDQUIST, E. F. (1953) *Design and Analysis of Experiments in Psychology and Education*. Boston: Houghton Mifflin.

McCALL, G. J. and SIMMONS, J. L. (eds.) (1969) *Issues in Participant Observation: A Text and Reader*. Reading, Mass.: Addison-Wesley.

McLAUGHLIN, SISTER M. K. (1963) 'A Survey of Music Activities, Materials and Techniques for Teachers of Elementary Educable Mentally Handicapped Children'. PhD dissertation, Michigan State University.

McLEISH, J. (February 1968) 'The Validity and Reliability of Bentley's Measures of Musical Abilities', *Br. J. Ed. Psychol.*, 38, p. 201.

McLEISH, J. and HIGGS, G. (1967) *An Inquiry into the Musical Capacities of Educationally Subnormal Children*. Occasional Research Papers No. 1. Cambridge: Cambridge Institute of Education.

MINISTRY OF EDUCATION. (1954) 'The Training and Supply of Teachers of Handicapped Pupils'. Fourth Report of the National Advisory Council on the Training and Supply of Teachers. London: HMSO.

MINISTRY OF EDUCATION. (1961) 'Special Educational Treatment for Educationally Sub-normal Pupils'. Circular 11/61. London: Ministry of Education.

NATIONAL SOCIETY FOR MENTALLY HANDICAPPED CHILDREN. (1966) *Survey of Provision Made for Educationally Subnormal Children in the Counties of Anglesey, Caernarvonshire, Cheshire, Derbyshire, Denbighshire, Flintshire, Lancashire, Merionethshire, Westmorland, Isle of Man*. Manchester: National Society for Mentally Handicapped Children, North-West Region.

NOCERA, S. D. (April 1972) 'Special Education Teachers Need a Special Education', *Music Educators Journal*, 58, 73–75.

NORDOFF, P. and ROBBINS, C. (1965) *Music Therapy for Handicapped Children: Investigations and Experiences*. New York: Rudolf Steiner Publications.

NORDOFF, P. and ROBBINS, C. (1971a) *Therapy in Music for Handicapped Children*. London: Victor Gollancz.

NORDOFF, P. and ROBBINS, C. (1971b) *Music Therapy in Special Education*. New York: John Day Company.

O'CONNOR, N. and HERMELIN, B. (1963) *Speech and Thought in Severe Subnormality: An Experimental Study*. London: Pergamon Press.

PARLETT, M. R. and KING, J. G. (1971) *Concentrated Study: A Pedagogic Innovation Observed*. Research into Higher Education Monograph No. 14. London: Society for Research into Higher Education.

PARLETT, M. R. and HAMILTON, D. (1972). *Evaluation as Illumination: A New Approach to the Study of Innovatory Programs*. Occasional Paper 9. University of Edinburgh: Centre for Research in the Educational Sciences.

PFLEDERER, M. (1964) 'The Responses of Children to Musical Tasks Embodying Piaget's Principle of Conservation', *J. Res. Mus. Educ.*, 12, 251–68.

REACKS, B. (1961) 'Music as an Aid to the Teaching of Other Subjects', *Special Education*, 50, 3, 27–28.

RICHARDSON, M. W. and KUDER, G. F. (1939) 'The Calculation of Test Reliability Coefficients Based on the Method of Rational Equivalence', *J. Ed. Psychol.*, 30, 681–87.

ROBINS, F. and ROBINS, J. (1963) *Educational Rhythmics for Mentally Handicapped Children: A Method of Practical Application.* Rapperswil: Ra-Verlag.

ROETHLISBERGER, F. J. and DICKSON, W. J. (1939) *Management and the Worker: An Account of a Research Program Conducted by the Western Electric Company, Hawthorne Works, Chicago.* Cambridge, Mass.: Harvard University Press.

ROWNTREE, J. P. (1969) 'A Critical Evaluation of the Bentley "Measures of Musical Abilities", with Particular Reference to Practice Effect on Various of the Sub-tests'. MEd dissertation, University of Newcastle-upon-Tyne.

SCHMITT, SISTER C. (December 1971) 'The Thought-Life of the Young Child: Jean Piaget and the Teaching of Music', *Music Educators Journal*, 58, 22–6.

SCHOOLS MUSIC ASSOCIATION. (1964) 'Report on Music in Special Schools'. London: Schools Music Association.

SEGAL, S. S. (1972) *Mental Handicap: A Select Annotated Bibliography.* Slough: NFER.

SERGEANT, D. (1969) 'Pitch Perception and Absolute Pitch: A Study of Some Aspects of Musical Development'. PhD dissertation, University of Reading.

SHUTER, R. (1968) *The Psychology of Musical Ability.* London: Methuen.

SHUTER, R. and TAYLOR, S. (1969) 'Summary of Discussions: International Seminar on Experimental Research in Music Education, University of Reading', *J. Res. Mus. Educ.*, 17, 1, 32–38.

STANDING CONFERENCE FOR AMATEUR MUSIC. (1971) 'Music for Slow Learners: Bibliography 1971'. Dartington College of Arts, Totnes, Devon: Standing Conference for Amateur Music.

STENHOUSE, L. (1970/71) 'Some Limitations of the Use of Objectives in Curriculum Research and Planning', *Pedagogica Europea*, 6, 73–83.

TABA, H. (1962) *Curriculum Development: Theory and Practice.* New York: Harcourt, Brace & World.

TANSLEY, A. E. and GULLIFORD, R. (1965) *The Education of Slow Learning Children.* rev. ed. London: Routledge & Kegan Paul.

TAYLOR, L. C. (1971) *Resources for Learning.* Harmondsworth: Penguin.

TAYLOR, P. H. (1970) *How Teachers Plan Their Courses: Studies in Curriculum Planning.* London: NFER.

TERMAN, L. M. and MERRILL, M. A. (1961) *Stanford-Binet Intelligence Scale: Manual for the Third Revision Form L–M.* London: Harrap.

THOMAS, D. J. (1968) *A Guide to the Literature of Special Education.* Educ. Lib. Public. No. 2. University of Liverpool School of Education.

TODD, R. (1958) *Child Health and Paediatrics: For Nurses, Health Visitors and Social Workers.* London: William Heinemann Medical Books.

TYLER, R. W. (1949) *Basic Principles of Curriculum and Instruction.* Chicago: University of Chicago Press.

VERNAZZA, M. (April 1967) 'What Are We Doing About Music in Special Education?' *Music Educators Journal*, 53, 55–8.

WARD, D. (1970) *Music for Slow Learners.* Guide Lines for Teachers, No. 8. London: College of Special Education.

WARD, D. (1972) *Sound Approaches for Slow Learners*. London: Bedford Square Press.

WECHSLER, D. (1949) *Wechsler Intelligence Scale for Children: Manual.* New York: Psychological Corporation.

WINTERS, G. (1967a) *Musical Instruments in the Classroom*. Education Today. London: Longmans, Green & Co.

WINTERS, G. (1967b) *An Introduction to Group Music Making*. London: Chappell.

WISEMAN, S. and PIDGEON, D. (1970) *Curriculum Evaluation*. Exploring Education Series. London: NFER.

ZEAMAN, D. and HOUSE, B. J. (1963) 'The Role of Attention in Retardate Discrimination Learning'. In: ELLIS, N. R., (ed) *Handbook of Mental Deficiency: Psychological Theory and Research*. New York: McGraw-Hill.